THE LAST, BEST HOPE:

Eduardo Frei and Chilean Democracy

THE LAST, BEST HOPE:

LEONARD GROSS

Eduardo Frei &

Chilean Democracy

RANDOM HOUSE

NEW YORK

Selflessness is a precious, rare, elusive human treasure
that suffuses some of the principals in this story
as it does my mother, Clara S. Roer,
to whom, with love, I dedicate this book

THE LAST, BEST HOPE

Can Democracy serve modern revolution?
No question presses or eludes the Free World more,
and no better answer may be forthcoming than from Chile,
where Christian Democratic President Eduardo Frei
attacks four centuries of semifeudal despair,
yet hallows personal freedoms. Frei's failure could
throw Chile to the Marxists in 1970. His success could
charge a continent—and alert the revolutionary world.

ACKNOWLEDGMENTS

In the summer of 1960, the editors of *Look* asked me to prepare for publication a report by Adlai Stevenson on a trip he had recently made to Latin America. Editing Stevenson should have been a matter of fitting his text to the space provided. But this was a campaign year; Stevenson was pressed and preoccupied; the article lacked the minted quality that I had always associated with his work. In search of the trouble, I must have read the article twenty times. Each reading left me more excited—and more distressed. The technical problems could be uncovered and exorcised. The content was indelible and haunting.

Stevenson had titled his article "Our Plight in Latin America." In 5000 words he had organized the puzzle, at least, of a dangerously disordered world. In conclusion he had warned: ". . . the gap in communications between our continents must be closed. We have too little information about each other, and too much misinformation. For a month during my travels, I never saw an American newspaperman."

Our best journalists, like our first-string scholars and diplomats, had for the most part dismissed Latin America as a bad musical comedy, a political parody unworthy of serious concern. But to me, the problems Stevenson laid bare seemed as alive and vulnerable as human flesh. I found his challenge irresistible. When I asked my editors for time to develop story possibilities, the time was gladly given. Three weeks later, I offered a dozen suggestions. The next day, I received a one-word reply: "Fine." So began the most rewarding years of my professional life.

My gratitude, then, begins with Stevenson, who touched me, as he did so many others, in a way he never knew; it embraces as well *Look*'s great editor, the late Daniel D. Mich, who charged me with a special assignment that kept me constantly in South America during 1962 and 1963, and frequently there during several other years; and Gardner Cowles, *Look*'s founder, whose reverence for editorial independence has fostered the climate that enabled me to investigate and report, as I saw fit, even the most delicate aspects of Latin American social, political, economic and cultural life. For *The Last, Best Hope* I had to work far beyond my magazine assignments, yet each of those assignments contributed something to my preparation for the book.

Hundreds of Latin Americans, as well as North Americans working in the field, taught me the bittersweet lessons of that harsh yet enticing world—statesmen and revolutionaries, landlords and squatters, wise men and liars, dreary old mystics and determined child-realists. Some of those who helped most would want least to read their names; they will find satisfaction, I hope, in the impression their ideas made on my own. Because reporting, while fundamentally a matter of asking much of many, is ultimately a matter of knowing whom to believe, any blame for error must be my own.

The assistance of several persons must be specified,

whether they like it or not: Radomiro Tomić, Chilean ambassador to the United States; Enrique Bernstein, Chilean ambassador to France; Alvaro Marfan, friend and ally of President Frei; Renato Poblete, S.J.; Holley Bell, information officer of the United States embassy in Santiago; and my colleague Joan Henricksen who, to the extent of human capacities, purged this book of its sins.

To my wife, Jacquelyn, who helped greatly in the early stages of research, to my daughter, Linden, and son, Jeffrey, I offer apologies for my preoccupation, thanks for their patience and gratitude for their love.

Leonard Gross

Paris
May 1, 1967

CONTENTS

xiii

THE LAST, BEST HOPE:

Eduardo Frei and Chilean Democracy

Introduction

I met Eduardo Frei in March 1961. I had gone to Chile on what proved to be the first of six visits, and had been advised by a number of Chileans that there was a worthy senator, a Christian Democrat and presidential aspirant, who could help me put the country's affairs into perspective. He was, they said, keen and concerned.

Frei received me in his law office. It was a small, dark room looking onto a bleak interior court, hardly a setting of status, yet richly yielding, I would later realize, about the nature of the man. I was struck at once by his face, by its boniness, spareness and obvious nose, but mostly by its nakedness. Perhaps it was the eyes, so intent, so revealing, or perhaps the fluidity of the features. Whatever, it seemed the face of a man who could not hide.

Later, many times later, I would see this utterly solemn man break into the most abandoned of smiles, his head thrown back to let out a boisterous laugh. But now, as I explained my purpose, Frei looked at me so seriously that he almost seemed unhappy. At the outset I attributed his

THE LAST, BEST HOPE

concentration to an effort to understand me (that was the only time we ever spoke English together, and Frei's is not good), but before long I had the unmistakable feeling that though we were strangers, Frei was as concerned about me, personally, as he was about my question. Whatever his earlier preoccupation, it was now cast from his thoughts; for him, in that moment, I was the most important person on earth.

We discussed the general state of Chile—the economy, the inflation, Chile's chronic dollar shortage, her need to import food, her overreliance on a single export commodity, copper. And we discussed politics. The Communists, outlawed between 1948 and 1958, had recently made a stunning comeback, and I had encountered some speculation that the party might actually elect a president in 1964. When I asked Frei to comment, he first asked me not to quote him.* Then he said that the Communists could, indeed, elect a president. In the next few minutes he showed me how. Their coalition with the Socialists and other left-wing radical groups, which they dominated, had come within 33,500 votes of electing Socialist Salvador Allende, a doctor and senator, in the 1958 election—an election in which Frei had finished a distant third. Should the economic program of the present government fail, as Frei expected it would (and as it later did), and should the Cuban experiment succeed, Allende could, said Frei, win the presidency in 1964.

In 1964 it was not Allende who won. It was Frei. The manner of his winning was as striking as victory itself. For the first time in modern Chilean history a candidate had received a majority of the popular vote. Normally, three or more candidates share the vote so evenly that Congress

---

* A restriction he later removed.

must choose between the top two. The broad political division had always been a rich indication of Chile's inability to agree upon national goals. Now Frei, with 56 percent of the vote, had a mandate for action.

The world of Latin American affairs is populated by men for whom frustration is all but endemic. Even as they fight for change they gird for failure. They have been failed before. On occasion they have been used, even cheated. These men—diplomats, technicians, scholars, chroniclers—witness life as a series of promises passionately given, capriciously forgotten.

Yet today many of these cautious men are aflush with hope. In the emergence of Eduardo Frei Montalva they recognize a rare moment in the evolution of Latin America. They believe that Frei's heralded "revolution with liberty" could transform Chile into a viable modern society. Conceivably, the Chilean experience could inspire the Southern Hemisphere.

Nationals of other Latin American countries don't like to admit it, but Chile has been a hemispheric leader out of all proportion to her size. Chile filtered Europe's contribution to Latin American culture, adapting and translating it to New World terms. Chileans instructed by Germans helped train the Colombian, Venezuelan, Paraguayan and Salvadoran armies. Influenced by Germans and Frenchmen, Chile was the first Latin American republic to establish a system of public education, to have a national teachers college, and to provide higher education for women, and Chileans helped design educational plants or provided technical assistance in education for a dozen Latin American countries. Chile's experts dominate many international agencies. Chile was the first Latin American country to organize her own development agency (several countries now have agencies modeled along Chilean lines), the first to organize politically, the first to permit a popular front, the first to cope realistically with diverse political elements that other Latin American countries smother today at their peril.

Latin America is strikingly susceptible to cyclical change. A successful military coup d'état in one country will often induce attempted coups in others; a surging political organization rallies like-minded groups throughout the hemisphere. Already several governments have sent study groups to assess the Chilean adventure. "They may not like Chile," notes a veteran student of Latin America affairs, "but they are always deeply interested in what goes on in Chile."

The case for Frei and Christian Democracy, as well as its potential for Latin America, has been efficiently summarized in the abstract of an address to the American Academy of Political and Social Science by the indefatigable *New York Times* foreign correspondent, Tad Szulc:

> If certain observable trends in Latin America continue, Christian Democracy could well become the political dimension that Latin America at its present stage of development requires. Although a great social, economic, political and psychological revolution has been sweeping Latin America, no political ideology has arisen with it. Most political parties have been convenient umbrellas for various, shifting small interest groups. Aside from a few strong parties in individual countries, political parties have lacked purpose and have shown ideological weaknesses. Although communism and socialism have been influential on occasion and in different countries, neither has managed to become the party of the masses. The two clashing influences of the present age in Latin America—the Cuban Revolution and the Alliance for Progress—created the need for a solution of their conflict. Christian Democracy, especially as it has emerged in Chile, with the resounding success of President Eduardo Frei Montalva, offers hope of a synthesis. Its ideas appeal to

6

youthful intellectuals and to middle-class women, and it has the support of the Roman Catholic Church and the labor unions. . . . Although political predictions are risky, we cannot ignore the significance of the new trend toward Christian Democracy in Latin America.

Eduardo Frei has been anything but ignored. In July 1965 he traveled to Europe on a good-will mission; his welcome was unprecedented for a Latin American leader. "Visiting chiefs of state are a dime a dozen on the Continent," wrote the usually unimpressionable *Visión Letter*, a weekly publication on Latin American affairs. "Paris has hosted twenty-one so far this year. The enthusiasm of Frei's reception was, therefore, extraordinary and profound." In Rome, Pope Paul VI praised him for "carrying out the wise transformation of structures that the rhythm of the times demands." In Paris the imperious Charles de Gaulle granted him three private interviews and offered several lavish parties. The London *Times* hailed Frei as "the most significant political figure in Latin America today." Everywhere he went the words were like these: "A new wave . . . a new hope . . . the new man of Latin America." After twenty-four days Frei returned to Chile. More than 100,000 Chileans braved chill winter rains to cheer the smiling, tearful president on his trip from Los Cerrillos Airport to the palace in the center of the city. "The trip has doubled his authority," a former Chilean diplomat calculated. "The Chilean didn't realize the kind of man he had elected, and what his height really was."

Vivas sang out for Frei throughout the Southern Hemisphere. The *New York Times* reported: "The impact on Latin America as a whole of President Eduardo Frei Montalva's trip to Western Europe appears to be as important as its impact on Chile." A U.S. official, one of Frei's legion of admirers at the operations level of the State Department, privately summed up the prayerful expectations of his colleagues: "He has a supranational dimension. He will be known years hence as one of the initiators of a Latin American alliance. This will be his legacy, even more than what he might do for Chile."

Even the most perfunctory understanding of Frei explains the praise and faith he arouses. Set against the historical image of the Latin American politician, his own glimmers. The traditional image portrays an autocratic, often coarse, frequently rich, opportunistic man. Frei is middle-class, dogged, restrained, intellectual. The image yields egocentricity. Frei, who prefers "we" to "I" in speeches, believes his party could do very well without him. I recall an overflow meeting of Christian Democrats in Viña del Mar in August 1963. Frei entered during the proceedings and stood, patient and unnoticed, with the crowd at the door. Only when the speaker had finished did he move forward to the platform—and bring the assembly, cheering, to its feet.

Traditionally, the Latin American official is ceremonious; Frei is uncomfortable at formal functions. The traditional official has an expansive view of right and wrong; Frei is immaculately honest. But for his principles, he might have been the president of Chile in 1958. According to many accounts, Frei could have secured the pivotal support of the Conservative party simply by requesting it in a letter. Frei refused to send the letter. "After twenty years of fighting, am I going to give up to the Right?" he asked me rhetorically once. "If I had sent that letter, I would have been president of the Right."

It was not the first time that Frei had acted on principle and against his interests. In January 1946, when he was the minister of public works, a strike of workers paralyzed the country. The government reacted vigorously against the

8

strikers—too vigorously for Frei's taste. He resigned. "It didn't assist either my career or my personal problems," he reflected recently. Eleven years later, circumstances dictated an opposite decision. Students were rioting in protest over increased bus fares. President Carlos Ibáñez asked Congress for special police powers. The political Left felt that government force had already exacerbated the situation. The political Right characterized the riots as revolutionary and supported Ibáñez. Frei voted with the Right, not because he agreed with its interpretation, but because he believed that a president must be permitted to govern, that lawlessness cannot be countenanced and that a clash between principle and politics must be decided in favor of principle. Criticism from his own party left Frei unmoved. Politics, he observed, is valid only to the point where it threatens integrity.

For the professionals, then, there are firm signs that with Frei a promise made will be a promise honored. But what excites them almost more than Frei's morality is his intellect, and the manner in which it perceives the Latin American problem.

"This movement means, in the first place, a breaking with the 'established order,' with prevailing structures," he declared in a speech. ". . . I would say that its central tenet is belief that we are witnesses to the crisis of a world exhausted; the death of paternalism and the birth of a civilization of work and solidarity with man as its center. . . . If being with the people, the workers, the poor in their struggle for justice, is to be on the Left, then undoubtedly we are there. Our first duty is with a world emerging in history, in search of a path and an expression."

Frei's own expression is luminous. Once, during our conversations together, he delivered a passionate, yet precise explanation of why he had sought a "third way":

There are two principal roads—capitalism and communism. Neither suffices because neither understands the sacred quality of man. Man *is* sacred. He is greater than the system. He has the right to life, to liberty and to his own personality. No system has the right to deprive him of his rights. But both principal systems do this, in one way or another—capitalism by dehumanizing him, by making his work the overpowering feature of his life, and communism, by making the good of the state superior to the good of the individual. A life of liberty is immutable. No society has the right to deny me the right to be myself. If I am nothing and the state is everything, the state denies me my rights as a personality. If 99 percent of the society says I have no right to be myself, I have the right to be against society. This is a conception of the individuality of man based in the idea that man is a creature of God, possessing a soul, and therefore transcends human structures.

For Frei, Christian Democracy not only confirms the uniqueness of man, it does so in universal terms. "Christian Democracy is a nonconfessional party, and it is not constituted by Catholics for Catholics," he explained in an address at the University of Notre Dame in 1963. "Because its principles are inspired by a philosophy which in the end is confirmed by natural right, its call goes to all—Catholics, people of other faiths or with none at all. Acceptance of its program is sufficient to belong to it. Indeed, in my country many Protestants, Jews and agnostics have joined Christian Democracy, and their company does us honor."

Two episodes during the first seventeen months of Frei's administration strongly suggested that the unusual qualities he reflects were translatable into solid political substance. Both were landmarks in modern Chilean history.

In March 1965 the Christian Democrats, deeply worried about the outcome, offered their candidates for Congress to the people. True, Frei had won the presidency, but a telling portion of his margin had been supplied by conservatives who perceived him as the lesser of two evils. Now, tradition held, the conservatives would return their old favorites to Congress, thereby hobbling Frei in his quest for reforms.

The results amazed conservatives and liberals alike. In heavy voting, the people more than tripled the Christian Democratic representation in the 147-seat Chamber of Deputies, giving the party eighty-two seats. For the first time in 124 years, an administration had a majority in the Chamber. Of the twenty contested seats in the Senate— there are forty-five in all—the Christian Democrats won twelve. So great was their voting strength that had they presented another candidate from Santiago, he too would have been elected. The measure of their surprise was that they had considered the possibility unworthy of a try.

In the postelection analysis, the accolades went to Frei. "It was not the Christian Democrats who won the election in March," said an observer. "It was Frei who won the election in March. 'A parliament for Frei,' was the slogan. You give the man a chance, particularly when he is talking and acting like Frei is talking and acting." And another: "He is a master strategist. He sold his determination to move ahead."

To the professionals, the second episode was of even greater import. The more cautious of his assessors, while acknowledging his intelligence and integrity, had tended to look upon these qualities as potential handicaps in the earthy arena of politics. Frei, they would often say, was constitutionally incapable of the elbowing and infighting that characterize political jousts. Yet, they argued, just such skills were required if Frei was to win in the Chilean Senate, where his own supporters were badly outnumbered.

The test began almost at once. The cornerstone of Frei's

1 1

program was an electrifying innovation—a partnership between the government of Chile and American-owned copper companies. For years U.S. firms in Chile had paid generous taxes and provided work for thousands of Chileans,
but had ultimately removed a good portion of their profits
from Chile. Now Frei proposed a greatly expanded joint
attack on copper, Chile's major dollar earner. With more
dollars, the country could guarantee the foreign exchange
needed to finance a growing economy.

The idea thrilled the experts. Not only did a partnership
make excellent economic sense, it might all but eliminate a
deeply felt political problem inherent in the American
presence abroad that Yankee "imperialists" were enriching
themselves at the expense of the poor. The Frei program
was almost too good to be true, and as the skeptics had
predicted, the foes of Frei marshaled forces to make certain it would be undermined. Critics on the Left and Right
cried that Frei was giving away Chile's resources. Debate
raged, strategists maneuvered, and at one point the cause
seemed so hopeless it provoked a rumor that should his bill
not pass, Frei might resign.

Then, fifteen months after it had begun, the battle ended
abruptly. The legislative cornerstone, chipped and scraped
but otherwise intact, settled into place. Once again the
credit went to Frei. His adroit, ceaseless behind-the-scenes
maneuvers now made him seem not simply an inspiring
Kennedy, but an effective Johnson.

And Chile, at last, seemed on the move.

To anyone who cares about the cold war, or communism
or our relationship with Latin America, Chile is an imperative study today. She is at a moment unlike any other in

Latin American history. The rust of centuries has been scraped away. For the first time a true opportunity exists to break away from the past. To misunderstand this moment, to misread the Chilean timetable, could cause great harm.

The gathering legend of Eduardo Frei is thus both a blessing and a curse: a blessing because it affords relief from the depressing defeatism that has characterized our modern relations with Latin America; a curse because it encourages the simplistic deduction that Frei's victory assures the Marxists' defeat. Nothing could be further from the truth, and Frei, more than anyone, knows this. "If this government fails, we're going to have a government of the extreme Left," he told me in August 1965, adding for emphasis, "of that I am sure." At the moment he spoke Frei had five years to prove to his people that reforms in a democratic context could vitalize Chile. And at that moment victory was anything but assured. Despite his mandate, the opposition from traditional elements in Chilean society was formidable. The conservatives, Frei said, simply did not understand that should he fail, the Chilean people would choose a more drastic experiment at their first opportunity. *"Para no perder unos pesos hoy, van perder las cabezas mañana,"* he said. "In order not to lose some coins today, they're going to lose their heads tomorrow."

Events soon gave literal meaning to his figure of speech. Chile's Marxists, spurned at the polls but far from crushed, had followed textbook tactics and turned to the picket line. One Marxist-controlled union after another either struck, engaged in slowdowns or threatened action. The most serious strike was in copper, which cost Chile an estimated $30 million in foreign exchange. Copper miners demanded wages two and one-half times in excess of the increase sanctioned by the government under its program to arrest inflation. Observers saw in the tactic an effort by Marxists to sabotage the Frei administration's overall economic plan, and thereby create the dissatisfaction that would enable them to gain power in 1970. No one foresaw the tragic consequence of the tactic: a battle in March 1966 between a thousand illegal strikers and a hundred soldiers and armed police at the Anaconda Company's El Salvador mine; eight died, dozens were wounded.

As Eduardo Frei completed his second year in office, it was at last evident that problems centuries in forming would not dissolve overnight.

It is only natural that we tend to minimize the past. Our era is so besieged by miracles that we have difficulty maintaining our bearings in time, let alone our perspective in history. It was little more than forty years ago that a young aviator sat in his airplane on a dark field near New York City, impatiently awaiting the first faint streaks of dawn—his signal to race the sun to California. By the mid-1970's, we will be making the same race daily and commercially, not against the sun but against the clock, and we will win with ease, roaring from New York's Kennedy International Airport at 8 A.M. and touching down at San Francisco International Airport at 7:45 A.M., local time.

The same factors of speed and distance that are so profoundly altering our lives are also altering our perspective on Latin America. Thirty years ago a flight to South America—for those who dared—might take a week. Two-motored DC-3's would pick their way carefully through Mexico and Central America, stopping each night to rest their weary passengers. Today's four-motored jets followed the brave line across oceans from New York to Buenos Aires in eleven hours, nonstop. Within a few years, supersonic jets will cruise at speeds that will make a journey to South America seem as simple as the shuttle flight from New York to Washington. Then our travelers will discover that the bulls of Bogotá charge as truly as those of Madrid, that Lima boasts one of the great restaurants of the world, that August skiing at Portillo matches the best February conditions in the Alps and that once a year in Rio de Janeiro the *cariocas* take temporary leave of their superegos while they dance themselves into madness.

But space-dwarfing speed is not simply a traveling convenience or a vehicle to thrills. It is an irresistible force for change. The swifter man's reach, the more complex his life, yearn though he might for simpler times. For North Americans, speed will rend the last remnant of isolation; it will relate us irrevocably to our hemisphere; it will make unbearable the absurd contradiction between the shining twentieth-century miracle cutting the sky to size, and the great craters of sixteenth-century misery slipping beneath its wings; it will provide us an unsparing view of Latin America, the modern anachronism, full of promise, yet empty of fulfillment, ripe with chance, yet rotten with failure, settled along its tempting fringes, untried in its forbidding interior.

Less than ten years ago we felt secure and happy with our assumptions about Latin America. We were the protector of a hemisphere, the model for inferiors. We took their raw materials and returned them as finished goods they were incapable of creating themselves. We organized defenses and wrote treaties for our mutual good. We were such Good Neighbors that we even had had a policy proclaiming as much.

What happened to these assumptions is history already

dangerously familiar. In Lima, a man stepped from a jeering crowd and spat on Vice President Richard M. Nixon; in Caracas, students stomped his car. Throughout the hemisphere our critics uttered outraged cries. They had been crying always. This time we listened.

The United States, they said, had lavished its technical and financial resources on Europe, and all but ignored Latin America. The United States wished to maintain Latin America as a supplier of cheap raw materials and a market for expensive manufactured goods. The United States made huge profits from its subsidiaries in Latin America but sent all the money home. The United States, callous and material, did not understand its spiritual, intellectual neighbors.

Our comfortable suppositions about Latin America had been supported by a façade of development. We saw glittering cities with distinctive styles, streams of cars flowing down avenues wide as a broad river, new universities, hospitals, construction. But the cries of anguish opened our eyes. We saw that much of this building was the leaf of an inflationary hedge; the scaffolds were often as empty as the reserves to complete the job; the cars were old American discards; the cities were ringed with slums; governments were confused or corrupt, plans were vague or nonexistent. And we saw in the political turbulence and instability and the intense talk of the revolutionaries an incredible possibility—that while we were diking East and West against the Communists, the Red tide could sweep our southern flank.

We are a pragmatic people. When we see something broken, we want to fix it. Seeing the state of disarray in Latin America, we set about to put it in order.

We saw, correctly, that it was not simply a matter of

repairing a broken vehicle. The need was to build a new engine of change. We drew up the blueprint for this new engine—the Alliance for Progress—and in a hail of good will we set out to build it.

It is still being built, and it will not be—could not be—completed for years. Yet within months after the Alliance was a fact, it was widely considered a failure. That judgment was as absurd as many of the assumptions with which the Alliance had been launched.

We had applied North American standards of logic to Latin American problems without realizing that a pragmatic attack almost invariably leads to a style and solution from which the Latin American recoils. We had assumed that because change was necessary, change would occur. We had not properly evaluated the tenacity and resistance of the forces against change: those Latin Americans for whom life was quite fine, old-fashioned, perhaps out of the mainstream, but serviceable nonetheless. We North Americans were perfectly agreeable to changing this order of life, but we had neglected to consider the proposition from the viewpoint of those who stood to lose.

Even here we erred. We applied dangerously common explanations to the resistance we encountered. Conservatism, we said. Oligarchic rule, we said. These are descriptions. They are not explanations. They do not suggest *why* these situations—true enough in some cases—exist, and they do not, therefore, instruct us in overcoming the problems.

Place yourself briefly in such a country. What would you do with your money if you thought your country was going socialist? Would you maintain your investment, mindless of the possibility that it might vanish through confiscation? Or would you send some of it to a numbered account in Switzerland as insurance against the time when you and your family might be forced to abandon your country? Would you pay taxes honestly if you knew that your money would finance needless jobs for friends of politicians or be administered by a tax collector whose salary was $100 a month, but whose home, which you passed each day on your way to work, was better than your own? Should entrepreneurs in a country in the initial stages of development pay high taxes? Our present income tax did not begin until 1913, years after our industrial base had been formed.

Actually, none of the arguments is ultimately persuasive. Each can be answered. The Latin American should pay taxes. What is important to know is that he will not pay because of a moral imperative to do so; his avoidance derives from profound cultural factors.

Many other misconceptions have hindered our coming to terms with the reality of Latin America in recent years. Not out of maliciousness, but simply because of a parochial viewpoint, have we failed to see perceptively.

Consider slums. We tend to view them as products of indifference, as proof that a segment of society is not well motivated, does not move even when helped, because it does not wish to help itself. There is another way to look at slums. They can be viewed as signs of earnestness, effort and hope. Many of the slums of Latin American cities today are products of the last fifteen to twenty-five years. They have been made largely by migrants from the countryside and mountain ranges. These people are on the move because they are seeking. They want work. They want to be near schools and hospitals. They want electricity and plumbing. They know from experience that they get none of these by remaining where they are. Our genuine pragmatists, they come to the cities, seeking.

18

I have made frequent visits to the homes of such people over the years. They are proud of their homes; often they prefer them to apartment houses set up by their governments. The apartments might offer advantages in comfort, but they would not belong to the occupant. The slum dweller treasures the idea of ownership. It is hard to imagine treasuring a shack of castoff lumber, but when you've never had anything, treasure is relative. The interiors of these shacks reflect this pride. Beds are made, dishes clean and stacked. The floors may be of dirt, but they are swept. The above description may apply to only a minority of slum dwellers, but they are real people nonetheless, and our concept of reality must be enlarged sufficiently to include them.

Trying to think and operate with real appreciation for another's viewpoint is a style that takes some getting used to. Much of our foreign policy has been based on humanitarianism, but much has also been designed for reasons of calculated self-interest. When we think in terms of our welfare, we call it "enlightened self-interest." When some other country does it we call it "nationalism." While it's perfectly true that nationalism captured by unhealthy political elements can be dangerous, it is equally true that nationalism can represent an opportunity. Whatever else it might be, nationalism is an awakening of pride; it produces a quickened effort. A brief reading of our own history during the late-nineteenth century would reveal a nationalism as fierce and protective against domination by foreign capital as any now existing in Latin America.

What are our own objectives in Latin America?

We have an emotional objective. We would like to win a victory in the greatest political battle of our time—democracy versus communism.

We have a practical objective. We want to be utterly

THE LAST, BEST HOPE

certain that not one inch of ground is given up to powers that would do us harm.

Finally, we have a humanitarian objective. We would like to help 225,000,000 persons find themselves, their century, their lives.

Our three objectives can only be realized by answers that serve the Latin Americans and bring them to terms with their own reality. Clearly, these solutions will not look like our own. They challenge our thinking. They may even have labels that frighten us. Yet they work. Using other words, other forms, yet retaining a firm grasp on the dignity and freedom of the individual, they achieve solutions.

Eduardo Frei is not simply the culmination of a set of historical forces in Chile. He is the latest, freshest, strongest example that Latin America could find itself, on the democratic Left.

The *raison d'être* of democratic reform movements is that in the fight against communism, the Right is bankrupt and powerless. The people are not interested in a continuation of what exists; what exists clearly does not provide for them. They want change. It is the democratic Left that embraces change in the context of respect for individual liberty and marries the idea of reform to the idea of freedom.

Communists do not fear the Right; they know that they can defeat it. They do fear the democratic Left, for they have tasted defeat several times at its hands. The democratic Left preempts the Communists' position on reform; nothing hurts the Communists more.

Chile today offers a classic test of whether Latin America has the capacity to create a "third choice" between communism and reaction. Chile is a microcosm of all that is wrong in Latin America. Its struggle suggests not what will happen (for it is impossible to predict that in Latin America), but what *ought* to happen. If Frei and Chile fail, the future for democracy in Latin America will seem grim.

Many say that the countries of Latin America cannot be lumped together, that, in fact, there is no such thing as Latin America. Comparisons anger and even enrage Latin Americans, for the differences among the countries are palpable. Peru, Ecuador and Bolivia, with their numerous Indians, or Brazil, with its Negroes, can hardly be likened to Argentina, with its Spaniards, Italians and Germans. Colombian aggressiveness cannot be likened to Brazilian softness or Chilean doggedness.

But these differences aside, there are binding human problems. There is the problem of underdevelopment. Almost every Latin American country earns its foreign coin from one chief product: bananas in Central America and Ecuador; coffee in Colombia and Brazil; tin in Bolivia; oil in Venezuela. In Chile the product is copper, but copper is no more enough than coffee, tin or bananas.

There is the problem of overpopulation. Latin America tamed disease in this century. Until then, malaria, yellow fever and smallpox had masked a propensity to reproduce unequaled in the world. Today the population of most Latin American countries is increasing at a rate of 3 percent a year. Should present trends continue, the population, some 225,000,000 today, will reach 600,000,000 by the end of this century. It is not that there isn't room; there is more room in Latin America than anywhere else in the world save Africa. The problem is that Latin America has not yet shown any capacity to support its *present* population. An unrestrained birth rate at this juncture could create a human catastrophe by the year 2000.

There are the inherited cultural problems implicit in

Hispanism and Catholicism. The Latin American may not be as mystically, culturally or violently Spanish as the Spaniard, his dreams not so lofty, nor his flights so fancy, but he retains a Spanish temptation to retreat from reality, a gracious trait in another world but a fatal weakness in this. "*Lo mejor de la vida es la ilusión*," reads the neat, flowered placard on the cab driver's dashboard: "Illusion is the best thing in life."

The final problems are those that bind Latin Americans to one another, as well as to the rest of the world—the human problems of doubt, worry, lack of belief, cynicism, envy, contempt—each the consequence of centuries of defeat, each a factor as real and debilitating as material deficiencies themselves.

Latin America may not be a place, but it is a condition—whose symbols might well be the uncompleted building, the abandoned project, the crippled dream. Too often the needs of its people are in conflict with the imagined rights of the individual, and too often, therefore, little or nothing gets done.

The problem of Latin America is not, ultimately, underdevelopment; it is not poor natural or human resources. It is the problem of despair. The Latin American must find his own solution, not simply because his problems are distinctive, but because the act of conquest itself provides psychological confirmation that he can function in the modern world.

Chile today serves Latin America as a laboratory in which weaknesses may be analyzed and strengths discovered. Out of Chile could emerge a chemistry of success.

1

The Quiet Country,
the Distant Corner

A freak, they have called her, a wrinkled pea pod, a withered bean. She is none of these. She is lovely—thin and long, yet lovely; wrinkled and craggy in places, yet lovely.

Hard, bare, tawny lovely in the North, where the earth is so sandy you expect camels but where there is almost nothing: not trees or grass, because there is no rain; not people, except in the infrequent towns where the first wave of Englishmen toasted their new mining fortunes with more champagne than was consumed per capita anywhere else in the world, and thinking they had sacked the earth, moved on. They were wrong. On this upper third of Chile, strewn with bizarre, wind-fashioned forms, are signs rich to the practiced eye. Twice in a hundred years men have seduced from these soils great mineral riches, first of nitrates, now of copper. ". . . This is a magic desert," one man has written, "a wasteland possessed of infinite riches which

men have given their lives to discover and whole armies
have fought to secure. . . . The very lack of rain, which
means that no vegetation can grow, nor animal life exist,
has led to the formation of chemicals which elsewhere are
washed out of the earth and lost."

Cruel, twisted, wind-ridden lovely in the South, where
Germans and English and Scots speak Spanish and raise
sheep with the thickest coats imaginable, and where the
pay is double what it is in Santiago to lure the teachers and
doctors and engineers to the hard land. But the broom
blooms there as in Scotland, stands of cool, shady pines
bend to the winds for a thousand near-silent miles, the white
glaciers loom like monarchs over the cold lakes, and a man
turns humble as he senses his own impermanent place in
time.

And finally, there is the loveliness of central Chile, "an
infinitely green and pleasant land," which shelters and provides for two-thirds of all Chileans, most of them in and
around Santiago. This central valley, so evocative of the
Mediterranean and of California, cooled by winds from the
Peru Current, explodes fruits and flowers from deep, rich
topsoil. At the edge of the valley, never out of sight, rise
the soaring mountains. Winters they gather a delicate
snow; summers they send the snow, first slowly, then headlong, down the wrinkles, the aged lines; the waters gather
speed, become falls, then cascades, finally slowing to
streams and rivers that nourish the fields of wheat, barley,
rice, corn and melon, the orchards of peaches, plums, or-
anges and cherries, and, of course, the vineyards whose
grapes yield sturdy wines that are not great but good, the
whites dry and tangy, the reds smooth but not heavy, wines
that are used mostly well, but too often to escape from sad-
ness.

For Chile is the end of the world, not simply the geographic bottom, but isolated on one side by 2650 miles of ocean and on the other by the Andes, the longest mountain range in the world. It is a mistake to overvalue geography as a forge of character; it is also a mistake to ignore geography altogether. This dominant spine of mountain that shelters Chile burdens her 8,500,000 people with a sense of remoteness and isolation. "Since you are born," says the handsome young Chilean, "you know you are in a quiet country—a country that has been quiet for almost 150 years." Being Chilean involves a degree of reflectiveness almost totally foreign to our headlong, committed world. It breeds a detached presence, an intuitive sense that whatever is to happen must happen from within. The Chilean's isolation has made him a careful, meditative man. But his thought lacks range.

Isolation binds Chileans to one another. "I always feel at home in Chile," boasts a young Chilean man. "North or South, I can stand on a street corner and yell, 'Hey, *amigos!*' I'm a member of a community that is united." The rough texture of the land has its impact too. "In Argentina," says one Chilean, "it rains and you have everything you want, but in Chile you have to fight against nature, against the mountains to make them produce." The Northerners, particularly, reflect this struggle. They are pushers, used to fighting the elements; they are simple and classless people as well, for their hard environment breeds equality. Southerners, mostly self-reliant and purposeful, are often moody and lonely. Wherever they live, Chileans are used to contact with nature, with lakes, mountains and willows, to a degree that makes them feel their human dimension. "The man in Chile is nothing compared to nature," Nemesio Antunez, the painter, observes. "It's dramatic. It can be gay. It can be tragic. It can be the softest place. It can be an earthquake."

This skinny land, almost grotesque-looking on a map, so beset by contrasts of length and width, height and depth, prune-faced in places, peach-smooth in others, hot and cold, calm and turbulent—this distant corner is today a focus of the world's gaze. In a hemisphere beset by change, revolution, turmoil, intrigue, Chile seems bent on order and skill. For more than a year she kept a sophisticated world marveling at her audacity—to decide by democratic process whether to submit to an authoritarian process. Always, everywhere, the choice had been imposed by brutal or subversive force. Now, here was a people determined to choose in freedom.

Chile arouses a sturdy emotion in most foreigners. While Brazil enraptures them and Argentina enrages them, Chile, for those who know her is the good friend: staunch, agreeable, steady, not so stodgy as such words imply, yet comfortably predictable, operating with values of universal worth. ". . . You note how people speak closer to your mind," V.S. Pritchett wrote of Chile after touring South America. "They do not stimulate the imagination by dramatic gulfs, but talk in the same way, read the same books, believe in the same things, enjoy the same jokes. . . . The formal señorita has given place to *la femme*; the secluded madonna to the married woman of active mind. She is often fair-haired, a vivid mixture of Northern and Spanish types, with quick nerves and freedom of manners."

Foreigners are forever comparing Chileans to other nationals. The English, for instance, call them the English of South America, perhaps because so many Englishmen have made Chile their home, or perhaps because the British navy has had a strong influence on Chilean maritime life.

But the educated Chilean, strongly cosmopolitan, compares himself to the French. He tells you that when a good Chilean dies, he goes to Paris. In Chile, French influence is apparent in the proliferation of political parties, the outlook of the Roman Catholic Church, the cuisine, the fashions. (But French influence is becoming dated. The son of a French-speaking Chilean speaks English, wears jeans and dances to the Yankee beat.)

Whatever influences have merged into the Chilean style, it is a style foreigners enjoy. Scattered through Santiago, which looks something like a European city at the foot of the Alps, are dozens of offices of international agencies. If there is a Geneva of Latin America, it is Santiago.

It is the warmth of the Chileans that seduces the foreigner. "At first encounter, Chileans appear somewhat reserved, even in comparison with the often grave Argentines," James Rowe, now of the American Universities Field Staff, wrote a few years ago. "On a little acquaintance, their natural qualities of friendliness and generosity are soon apparent. Hospitality is legendary. All over Latin America, the standard welcome one receives on entering a home is *es su casa:* 'This is your house,' an affable greeting about as specific as the New Yorker's 'Let's have lunch someday.' Chileans really mean it." At one dinner party a guest, a total stranger until that evening, insisted that Rowe move from his hotel to the man's home, where Rowe remained for the rest of his visit.

John Wood, now information officer of the Food for Peace Program in Washington, spent two years in Chile in behalf of the Alliance for Progress. On his last day at work he tried to clean up some odds and ends, to the increasing annoyance of his normally amiable secretary, who kept complaining that she was late for a luncheon appointment.

Finally she burst into tears and confessed that she could not stand to see Wood and his family leave Chile. Twelve Chilean families came to the airport to say farewell, bearing gifts of wine and *pisco*, the young, aggressive grape alcohol, and little gifts for the Woods' three children. After Wood had been back in the States for two months, I had lunch with him in Washington. He was suffering from an extreme case of reverse cultural shock. Americans, he complained, don't know how to eat. The waiters are surly. The women have no mystique. In Chile, he said, relaxation is an art, the enjoyment of other people a practice. "When you go to their homes for dinner, you are a member of the family for the night you are there. I can't get used to walking into the homes of close friends and not embracing them."

Most North Americans respond warmly to the Chileans. Two of them, Fredrick B. Pike and Donald W. Bray, explained why in an excellent article:

> In Chile [they wrote] there is a highly developed sense of decency and fair play. . . . The respect for freedom of expression and exchange of ideas seems at times more fundamental than in the United States. This is particularly noticeable in the broad diversity of opinions presented in the universities and in the press. Chileans, moreover, have a maturity, a self-containment, and an inner discipline which, combined with the rare willingness to think of adverse situations in terms of equally bleak alternatives, render them ill-disposed to rush to the barricades to defend momentary whims. To almost every political predicament except dictatorship they respond with patience and forebearance. In spite of their refreshing individualism, Chileans possess a deeply ingrained acceptance of authority and devotion to stability, a love of institutionalism and constitutional regularity. Their lively sense of humor enables them to respond to occasionally absurd political situations with laughter and with satire, rather than with rebelliousness of spirit. Chileans have de-

28

veloped a police force—the famed *carabineros*—that for integrity, efficiency and courteous firmness is unmatched in Latin America. And it is revealing that the populace continues to feel a sense of national guilt over the 1938 cold-blooded assassination of sixty-two youths who spearheaded an attempted Nazi revolution. Bloodier and less excusable acts have been readily forgotten elsewhere in the American Hemisphere, including the United States.

So much for warmth, for generosity toward foreigners, for national solidarity. There is a fascinating streak of meanness in the Chilean that expresses itself in many little ways. K. H. Silvert, a Dartmouth professor who once lived in Chile, has chronicled some of them:

> Pedestrians crossing the street deliberately dawdle and visibly dare car drivers to run them down. Elegantly dressed women use sharp elbows on buses and say nasty things should one try to make his way to the door at his stop. A courtesy extended to another driver on the road is so unexpected that it is liable to induce confusion if not collision. Never is a nod of acknowledgment or thanks to be expected. An entire day spent in Christmas shopping was brightened by not a single "thank you" from any salesperson. Unashamed breaking of queues is so common that embarrassing intimacies are caused in the attempt to allow no millimeter of opening as an invitation to hawk-eyed opportunists.

These extremes can be bound. Like most Latins, the Chilean has what one observer has charitably described as "a lively sense of his own situation." With family or friends he relates in a manner so genuinely passionate that most Anglo-Saxons would find it embarrassing. But beyond this small group he finds relationships uncertain, even threatening, and he develops no truly genuine feeling for strangers. A singular consequence is that Chile has no credit system to speak of. One sociologist observes: "If you have faith in one another, you have a good credit system." John Elac, a former Alliance for Progress aide who was born in Chile and spent most of his youth there, believes these hostile patterns can be traced to the competition for position that underlies Chilean life. "Everybody in Chile is trying to move up. You don't let others do you in, and since the best defense is a good attack, you do them in first. Chileans are sensitive not only to what everybody is doing, but to what they might be doing." Persistent inflation has sharpened this awareness. An American, once a resident of Chile, recalls: "In 1945 a Chilean would give his word and you didn't worry. But by the late fifties, the need for money drove individualism to an extreme." Some Chileans became corrupt from within.

With foreigners, or when he's abroad, the Chilean acts in a completely different manner, Elac points out: "He learns that he doesn't have to spend time defending himself." Chileans, he notes, are especially honest with non-Chileans, and for this reason do very well in international organizations.

There are other flaws in the Chilean character. While Chileans are noted for their respect for law and the democratic process, Chilean history is not without its blemishes. As recently as 1931, the country was controlled by a dictator; in 1957, student-led riots in Santiago caused some twenty deaths and hundreds of casualties. In 1965, authorities shot and killed several striking slum dwellers who had perched themselves on railroad tracks near a suburban Santiago *callampa*. Certain antisocial group characteristics found throughout Latin America exist in Chile as well. The evasion of taxes, the abdication of responsibility are both common. Lower-class Chileans drink too much as a rule, although less these days than formerly (since the institution of a bonus payment for faithful attendance at work), and are frequently given to incestuous relationships.

But faults are relative. If militarism is not unknown in Chile, it is not as readily accepted as elsewhere; if a streak of violence runs through the Chilean, he is nonetheless not as violent as, say, Colombians or Argentines or Venezuelans. Even dishonesty is not as prevalent in Chile as it is elsewhere. A Chilean with wide experience in international agencies once told me: "I think Chileans are the most honest people in South America. If you compare them with Brazilians, Peruvians, Ecuadorians, we are much better off. This may be due to the English influence. Most of us were brought up by nannies. Or it may be due to the Basque heritage of the ruling classes. The Basques, you know, were *the* class of Spain. Whatever it is, it's there. I'm an attorney, and I have never heard an intimation of a bribe in a tax case. In other countries, the captains of industry always expect a commission out of any business—something added onto the price of the deal that goes directly into the pocket of the captain. In Chile I have never heard of this. Politics? You know the tradition down here. You're in office, it's time to feather your nest. But look at our Radicals. They were in power many years. Not one of them who was in government was any wealthier when he left than when he entered."

What is striking about the Chilean, therefore, is that his bad traits are less incriminating than others', and that even though he has certain flaws in his character, he nonetheless *believes* that he is democratic, moderate, intelligent and mature. By believing, he enhances his chance of being so. The idea of a peaceful democratic choice between Marxism and democratic socialism—precisely the choice offered to voters in 1964—is unthinkable anywhere else in Latin

America. In other countries the organized forces would never have permitted the choice.

Whence comes this maturity? To a man, thoughtful Chileans, ruminating through history, arrive at the legacy of Diego Portales.

Few historical figures furnish a poorer democratic testament. Arrogant, cold, austere, with darting blue eyes and a sharp face, openly contemptuous of the common man, Hamiltonian in his belief that only propertied men should participate in government, Diego Portales ridiculed weak men mercilessly. He had a Machiavellian contempt for elective office; he revered only power. He could be cynically opportunistic. While his friends rode off to free Chile from the colonial domination of Spain, he secured a lucrative import monopoly on liquor, tea and tobacco. Before he was twenty-three, he was a wealthy man. This arrogant young man ruled Chile for eight years, beginning in 1829; though he never held elective office, he managed, nonetheless, to give the country its political shape and character.

It was his precocity that indirectly led him into government. He began trading at seventeen, and had secured virtual control of key imports six years later—control given him by the government; his actions aroused great public wrath. Angered by the abusive criticism, Portales decided that the people should have more respect for the acts of government, and set about to instill that respect.

He believed neither in democracy nor in republicanism, but in order. His motives could not have been more selfish, yet he saw correctly that rough political passions must be turned away from individual leaders and issues toward the institution of government itself.

He started one newspaper in Valparaíso and bought another in Santiago. He exhorted his readers to hallow government. His message was directed not at the *rotos*, or "broken ones," whom he despised, but at the vested interests who, lacking order, had played against one another to the destruction of all. Landlords, priests, militarists, businessmen, all felt the pressure of his will, yet saw as well that obedience could yield advantages.

His thought was simple enough. He wanted a strong, centralized government of men who were "models of patriotism and virtue. This government would extend itself as the ideas of these men permeated society." Again and again he preached that it was not the man but the office that must be revered. Had he used only editorials in his crusade, his cause might have been lost. But Portales knew how to back his words with action. First as minister of the interior, and later as minister of foreign affairs, war and navy, he gave policies of vigorous trade and governmental assistance to the businessmen; he gave the landowners assurances of family continuity of their estates; he gave the Catholic Church rights and privileges that had been lost under previous, more hostile administrations; he developed the Chilean Civil Guard; and he promoted loyal army officers who succeeded in court-martialing or exiling officers of a more rebellious mind.

For all his favors his price was the same—loyalty to the central authority. His ideas were finally given official form in the Constitution of 1833, which provided for a president to serve for five years, with the right to seek reelection once, and for two houses of Congress, both elected by literate male property owners over twenty-five. The constitution was not a democratic one; it did not enfranchise the majority of Chileans. But it did furnish a "habit" of government. And as the suffrage was extended it gave more and more people the habit of electing officials and instilled in them the belief that they could participate, to some extent at least, in a government that would respect their will.

It can always be argued whether the people made the habit, or the habit the people. Whichever, the fact is that Chileans are accustomed to seeing their elected officials take and leave office on schedule.

> In its political history [writes historian Hubert Herring], Chile has a record of stability unique in Latin America. Since 1830 presidents have [mostly] served their allotted terms . . . without the uprisings, unseatings, and assassinations which have been the rule in some other nations. A few Chilean presidents have ruled arbitrarily, but, since the days of Portales, dictatorships have been rare. At times political dissenters have been jailed or exiled, but they have never been submitted to sadistic torture or summary execution. Since 1833, Chile has lived under two constitutions, while most of the other [Latin American] republics have had a dozen or more. As an independent state, Chile has been relatively decorous and orderly, and during recent years, stoutly democratic . . . Despite the handicaps under which Chile labors, she stands as a notable stronghold of democratic conviction and practice in . . . Latin America. . . . There are abundant signs of vital enthusiasm for democratic institutions. The press is usually free, much of it is able, and most of it is committed to democratic institutions. The party system, chaotic as it is, gives evidence of democratic vigor. The Church, with some of the best-trained priests in Latin America, stands for social justice. . . . In spite of all the obstacles still to be overcome, Chile offers promise to the friends of democracy.

Herring also notes that Chile is "one of the four or five Latin American states in which elections are substantially honest and democracy is honored." If, as often happens, no candidate receives a majority of the vote, the election is turned over to Congress, which must then choose from the two candidates highest on the poll. Congress has always been able to select the second man, but it has never failed to elect the first.

Thus, at the time of the 1964 election, Chileans had a historical habit of democratic choice extending back 130 years. It was a habit that stood them well. In a real sense, their remarkable display of political maturity traces back to the arrogant young Portales. Could he somehow know now that hundreds of thousands of non-propertied Chileans had elected a president, he would be horrified. Yet Chilean democracy was forged on his will, as educated Chileans, the new president among them, recognize. "The world of Portales was fruitful," Eduardo Frei once wrote, "because it responded to our reality in his epoch."

And what was this reality? On the surface it was one of social and political disorganization, and that is undoubtedly what President Frei had in mind. But there was another problem, not present so much as feared—an inheritance of Spain and Spanish mysticism—a problem that Portales conquered probably without knowing what he was achieving. The problem is *personalismo*, a reverential attachment for leaders, an emotion to which Hispanic cultures are peculiarly addicted. The reason for this addiction relates powerfully to the Spaniard's mystical, intensely personal idea of God. A Jesuit priest, Roger Vekemans, has put the problem in clear general terms:

> To understand the Latin American Catholic, you must understand the relationship he feels to his God. Everything else flows from that. For him, God is a person; religion, therefore, is an exchange between two persons. This is as it should be in the religious sphere. But the Latin American carries this vision into the secular sphere, and here the problems begin.
>
> Consider the problem of authority. A Latin American puts a man in authority because he is a prophet and promises a certain salvation, and not necessarily because the man is

competent or even because he is the right man in the right place at the right time. He is in charge because he is a Messiah. Why? Because the Latin American personality stresses the relationship, political or otherwise, between a human being and some awesome, transcendent reality.

It is easy to see what a problem this fact presents to economic development that tries objectively to meet human needs. The President of the United States or the Prime Minister of Canada will listen to his economists and probably follow their advice, for Anglo-Saxon authorities are primarily interested in getting a job done. Latin American authorities do not, and in view of the Latin personality, cannot proceed so directly to the task.

It is the "lively perception of his own situation" that leads the Latin American not to political ideas that express a consensus, but to highly refined ideas that specifically meet his needs. Thus, political parties proliferate. In 1953 there were thirty-two in Chile—an indication that the tendency, if not its excesses, was present. And it is the Hispanic yearning for Messianic solutions that has produced the crippling demagoguery found so frequently in Latin America.

How much the control of this problem has meant for Chile can be seen by a comparison with her volatile neighbor, Argentina, whose passionate political divisions have once again disrupted the country. I recall a rally in 1963 for Juan Perón in Buenos Aires, the biggest permitted his followers by the government since his ouster in September 1955. Fifty thousand Argentines poured into a city square, pressing tightly against one another as they cheered, "Perón! Perón! Perón! Perón!" for the sybarite who had ruined his country, robbing the treasury to line his pockets and to buy votes, and thereby power. So intense was the emotion, so tightly did the *peronistas* press forward that at one point I thought I would be crushed. Finally the rally ended, the crowd ebbed, and I was able to make my way to a restaurant at the side of the square. As I composed myself at my table, I began to chat with a man nearby. I asked if he had been to the rally. He said that he had. I asked if he had been a *peronista*. He said that he had been, and that he still was. "Why?" I asked. "Because," he replied, "under Perón, life was good for *me*." That is the way he said it.

Personalismo runs like a fault through Latin America. By preaching a religion of government that would endure after the passing of men, Diego Portales drew his country from this Hispanic addiction. His concepts are woven into the texture of contemporary political life in Chile. The best evidence of this is Eduardo Frei himself. "I'm not important," he told me one day in 1963. "If it's not me, it will be someone else."

These are attitudes and habits we can rightly cheer. But it takes more than this to make a democracy.

Power

Technically, Chile is a democracy. Suffrage is widespread. All political parties have legal status. The press is free. Opinion courses through the universities and among thinking groups. A man may speak openly. The courts are independent. The celebrated Chilean police are trained to use a minimum of force. Military respect for civilian authority is unquestioned. Only three times in the last one hundred years has the military intervened in the civilian sphere; such intervention is all but unthinkable today. Thus, in key respects, Chile meets the test of a democratic society. Yet practically, what the Chileans have called democracy is simply not democracy as we know it.

For there are other tests of a democracy than freedom, the elective process and civilian autonomy. A democratic society, if it is viable, approaches an equality of possibilities through its laws. It functions in ways that create a climate for opportunity. It whittles away at social and economic extremes. Since this process does not occur naturally, there must be built-in devices that create mobility between the classes so that a man of the lower class who works and perseveres can prosper. But Chilean society is so rigidly structured that upward movement has been all but impossible for the overwhelming majority of Chileans. Those born poor remain poor. A man who has the right but not the strength to protest his hunger is only technically free.

K. H. Silvert, the American scholar, has set down an apt summary of the Chilean reality:

> Probably about a fifth to a quarter of all Chileans live in what we think of as a modern society: they are educated; they can aspire to higher position for their children without being unrealistic; they can talk and gather and write and read freely; they can make a fairly wide occupational choice; they have access to government and can be assured of equality before the laws; they can enjoy a wide array of the material fruits of industrial life; they can belong to unions and political parties and pressure groups and professional societies; and they can assume that their vote has some real significance. . . . This part of Chilean society is the effective nation. All public officials, military officers, intellectuals, professionals, bank clerks, storekeepers, industrialists, and large farmers are recruited from this limited but still significantly large segment. When we say "Chilean," it is almost certain that it is to them we refer, unless we specifically say *roto* (ragged man) or *inquilino* (tenant farmer) or *callampa* (shantytown) dweller. Certainly when we comment on the beauty of Chilean women we are not talking about the wives of farm workers; when we say that Chilean governors are sophisticated, or that the Chilean diet is French, we are not referring to the political choices of illiterate peasants or the food eaten by a construction worker in Chillán. Granted that we always use such selective perceptions in talking about societies, it is still useful to know that in Chile three-quarters of the population must be excluded from these generalizations.

Most concerned North Americans are reasonably familiar today with the generalizations that apply to this three-quarters of the population. Unless one has spent some time in such conditions, however, it is difficult to appreciate what these generalizations mean. The physical squalor may be imaginable—the dark, cramped quarters, the dampness and ugliness. What is all but unimaginable is the barrenness of spirit that hangs like fog about the degraded people who, cynical almost beyond redemption, do not believe in themselves. These people are found all over Chile, some still stirring the land, others drifting to the cities in a last desperate gesture, where they settle in *callampas*—so called because their wooden shacks sprout as rapidly as mushrooms. Perhaps the most humbling days of my life were spent in a *callampa* built atop a dump by workers whose principal means of salvation was to pick through the garbage piled next to their homes.

Many slum dwellers do find work. But the jobs they are fit for have until recently offered little more than the most marginal existence, and virtually no hope of advancement. Conditions have improved greatly in the last few years. Only a few years ago, however, they appeared bleak. At that time Joseph H. Fichter, a Jesuit sociologist, made a study of female domestic servants in Santiago, 93 percent of whom had migrated from rural areas.

> The conditions of work are arduous and the income is low [he reported]. For the majority (68 percent) of these women, the workday starts before seven o'clock in the morning, and ends after ten o'clock at night. The average number of daily working hours for all cases was 15.4 hours. . . . The average working week for a housemaid is 91 hours, 18 minutes; and in a thirty-day month (with two days off) she puts in 393 hours, 24 minutes. For this work she receives an average monthly take-home wage of 17.57 escudos.* [Fringe benefits

---

* About $16.70 in 1961.

increase pay by 50 percent; in most cases, the employer also provides room and board.] . . . upward social and occupational mobility for domestic servants is extremely difficult. Their household talents are not otherwise marketable, and their long working hours interfere with the development of other talents. . . . Nevertheless, there are some who have found an escape from domestic service. In one direction, it is the tragic estimate of the Santiago police that almost 70 percent of the city's prostitutes were formerly employed as housemaids; and it is the frequently voiced defense of these girls that "anything is better than being a house servant."

Chile continues to exhibit a fairly rigid class system, with an apparently built-in resistance to broad income distribution, to competitive achievement, to mass educational and occupational opportunities, and to social mobility. The case of the housemaids is one simple example of the obstacles to democratic development in a society which aspires to political sophistication but which maintains a closed social structure.

The manner in which Chilean workers are paid offers a fascinating comment on the domestic struggle for material advance, as well as the dichotomous quality of Chilean life. Conservative entrepreneurs rigorously maintain low wages, but they are also compelled to make "conscience" payments. The average pay of a skilled worker is about $75 a month. Mandatory bonuses, however, often double this figure. In addition to twelve monthly salaries, a worker may receive as much as eight months' extra pay, premiums for the zone he works in, for his travel, for each five years of work and for every change of residence. If a worker runs a machine he is paid especially for that. Holiday and overtime payments are standard. Even so, most salaries are substandard, and the average Chilean family requires two wage earners—or one with two jobs—to survive.

For the three-quarters of Chile's population who do not share in its fruits, democracy is simply an illusion. Fredrick

Pike states in his book, *Chile and the United States, 1880–1962*:

> Chilean political stability has been accepted as an indica-
> tion of conditions that are generally satisfactory to all ele-
> ments of society rather than as a miraculous manifestation
> of patience by vast elements of the population in the face of
> intolerable conditions. . . . The exclusion of so large a section
> of the population from actual participation in national devel-
> opment suggests that the much-heralded Chilean democracy
> is in many ways a myth.

How has a so-called democracy managed to create and
nurture such extremes? For some few years now, we North
Americans have been developing a simple and seemingly
satisfactory answer. We speak with assurance about the
fossilized, reactionary Latin American oligarchy, whom we
characterize as possessive, selfish men of extraordinary
wealth, capable of cruelty where necessary, and holding
sufficient power and control to maintain not only their
workers but also their countries in a state of virtual serf-
dom.

It is not that simple—not because the answer is necessarily incorrect, but because it is incomplete. The answer
does not suggest why or how such people, as generous and
charitable as any in the world, could allow such intense
suffering to continue. It does not examine the involved cultural, social and historical factors that have permitted
these conditions to flourish.

Any explanation must begin with a discussion of the
men who physically dominate the land, for their economic
power has enabled them to impose their views on the nation. Although such domination is frequently discounted
by the aristocracy, it is easily proved. Independent and
dispassionate studies produce approximately the same re-

42

sults: 9.7 percent of Chile's agrarian landowners hold 86 percent of the arable land; 74.6 percent own only 5.2 percent. In the rich central valley, the figures are even more extreme. There, in 1955, according to a study made by an American specialist, Marvin J. Sternberg, 1.1 percent of the owners held 72.7 percent of the total farmland, while 73.1 percent owned only 1.1 percent of this land. Generally, 1 percent of the agricultural population receives 25 percent of the annual income from agriculture, Sternberg calculated. "For the vast majority of the agricultural population," he noted, "the concentration of income means low wages and depressing poverty . . . poorly constructed and unhealthy housing, an almost total lack of sanitary facilities, contaminated water, poor nutrition, disease and an early death."

"Here has existed a New World country with the social organization of Old Spain," notes one historian, "a twentieth-century people still preserving a feudal society; a republic based on the equality of man, yet with a blue-blood aristocracy and a servile class as distinctly separated as in any of the monarchies of the Old World."

Historically, the paternal relationship between master and servant has been a powerful one: first, because the landowners frequently controlled the votes of their workers; second, because the relationship bred its own type of inertia. Father John J. Considine, a Maryknoll priest specializing in Latin American affairs, states:

> The *inquilino* is not bound to the land, legally or by custom. Yet he feels closely tied to it. He works land worked by generations of his family. His own family is attached to that of the *patrón*. He regards the estate as his protector. And the estate and its owner regard him the same way. The *patrón* feels very paternal about his worker. Within his understand-

ing of his obligations, he treats his workers well. But it is his understanding that is limited. He actually believes that the *inquilino* lives miserably because he is meant to. It is traditional. It is the order conceived by God. To change this way of life is not only impossible, it is undesirable. If the *inquilino* is given opportunity, he will leave the hacienda, and the hacienda will be destroyed.

The notion of reform has been anathema to the aristocracy. Until recent years, the *Sociedad Nacional de Agricultura*, an influential organization of landowners, had traditionally resisted all government attempts at reform. Only twenty years ago the society issued a position paper opposing reforms then being proposed, drawing this acid analysis from a Chilean writer:

> The proposal to set up inspectorates with powers to ensure that agricultural land is not unnecessarily neglected is branded as the death blow of private property. Legislation designed to penalize speculation and arrest the fatal course of inflation is a monstrous interference with legitimate profit. Even the obligation imposed on the great landowners to keep proper books and pay a very modest income tax is a disastrous and revolutionary innovation which they are resolved to resist to the last.

The society had, in years past, found the idea of syndicates, or unions, appalling:

> The syndicate is, without doubt, a false and illusory means of improvement for the workers, as experience shows. It only unsettles them and leads them astray. Their true advantage lies in their harmony with those in whose productive activities they share, in the same way as the advantage of the landlord lies in harmony with those who collaborate with him.

While the agricultural situation has improved in recent years, Chile has, in years past, literally had to pay for the traditional backwardness of many of her landowners. The deep soil of the central valley, watered by melting snows from the Andes, could yield far more food than it does; yet each year, of the $100 million Chile spends to buy food from abroad, $75 million is for food she could have produced herself. The process drained dollar resources, aggravated Chile's debt and burdened the Chilean laborer with high food costs that claimed between 60 and 80 percent of his earnings. Nutrition suffered. Even white-collar workers were compelled to substitute flour dishes for meat to a serious degree. At a time when Chile's food needs were increasing almost 3 percent annually, production was increasing but 1 percent a year. Over 60 percent of Chile's cultivated farmland was either left fallow or became pasture. Neither accident nor incompetence created this strange situation. It was caused by landowners, who, astonishingly, were disinterested in maximizing their yield.

A portion of this phenomenon yields to logic. Landowners argued that previous Chilean governments had, as a matter of political expediency, subsidized urban dwellers by depressing (or controlling) prices of agricultural products, and that they therefore were unable to earn a decent profit—in spite of government loans to them. But their charge has only a certain amount of validity. Controlled or "political" prices had only been in effect since 1938, and the inflation that provoked them could be said to have been caused, at least in part, by the policy of devaluation and tax-exemption, which the landowners had encouraged and profited from for years. Many well-to-do Chilean landowners, particularly those in the rich central valley, viewed their land in terms of the status it conferred upon the owner and had little interest in raising the productive capacity of their acres. The land served as a means of hiding wealth, or of securing a lower rate of taxation, or hedging against inflation or qualifying for credit at low interest rates, which in an inflationary society amounts to a gift.

In 1953 the United Nations investigated why farms in Latin America were doing so poorly. It discovered that in more than one-third of the cases, the principal reason was the owner's lack of interest. In Chile U.S. specialists sponsored by private foundations tried for years to interest landowners in modern farming methods. Few co-operated. Those who did produced far more than those who didn't— even though the land and personnel were almost identical in all cases.

When the traditional Chilean landowner did make a profit he would rarely plow his earnings into better equipment or other technological devices to increase production. Instead, he would invest the money in city-based industry and high-yield apartment buildings or spend the money on a trip abroad. Sternberg's study indicated that owners of big farms spent 99 percent of their disposable income earned from agriculture.

A second explanation of the stratification of Chilean society is political. For the oligarchy, politics has always been a form of insurance. Political considerations determine priorities for imports. A member of Congress can also use banking facilities to his advantage. In the United States almost everyone has access to credit. But in Chile, where credit is often difficult to obtain, political advantage can make it easier. So the Chilean oligarchy has always been well represented in Congress.

In the campaign of 1964 the oligarchy supported Eduardo Frei because it preferred him to the Socialist, Allende; but it did not support his program. In December 1964, shortly after the installation of Frei, a congressional

committee dominated by political conservatives returned
to the Chamber a bill for a "national solidarity tax" that
had been deemed "extremely urgent," contending that the
bill was not properly presented and should be redrafted.
The program called for new taxes on capital and property to
raise $100 million a year over the next five years to finance
additional rural reforms, communal development, education and housing projects. Said a *New York Times* dis-
patch: "Liberals and conservatives who had supported Mr.
Frei in the September 4 election despite his reformist platform, chided the government for attempting to create a
'crisis atmosphere' that was out of place in peacetime."

The attitudes of the oligarchy remain essentially the
same today as they were in the days of Portales. "A visit to
the eighteenth-century Santiago mansion in which the
Conservatives have their headquarters gives one the feeling of having an audience with Louis XIV," Pat Holt, a
staff consultant of the U.S. Senate Foreign Relations Committee, wrote a few years ago:

> Conservative leaders say quite frankly that the thrust of
> the Alliance for Progress is misdirected. It is a great mistake
> to advocate tax and land reform, because this simply stirs
> up people to demand changes which will upset the status quo.
> United States intentions are doubtless well-meant, but are
> based on a misunderstanding of the situation in Chile. In
> short, to paraphrase the Conservative attitude more bluntly
> than the Conservatives themselves state it: the people in this
> party have a good thing in Chile, and they don't want any
> crazy *gringos* trying to upset it. They are not even as per-
> ceptive as Louis XIV, who at least realized that the deluge
> was on the way.

This, then, is the old-fashioned Chilean elite, as bad as
its reputation in many respects, as shocking to many Chileans as it is to foreigners. Foreign critics are frequently

unaware that such men do not represent the Chilean majority or even the majority of the upper class. Numerous well-to-do Chileans, clustered to the Left and to the Right of the political center, would like to see control of the land removed from such men—just as they would like to see the country improve its industrial, commercial and educational processes. But they too are hampered in ways that inhibit change just as surely as does the mentality of the landed elite.

The majority of the Chilean upper class is civilized, urbane and agreeable. All of the pleasures for which we strive in our own society (and having earned them, find we have run out of time to enjoy them) are easily accessible to well-to-do Chileans.

There are few real fortunes in Chile; there is little need for them. An income of $20,000 a year is more than sufficient for a graceful life, with an excellent city home in the Barrio Alto, a weekend or vacation place at the shore or in the southern lake regions, and perhaps a *refugio* in the mountains near La Parva or Farellones, if the family skis.

The homes of the rich in Santiago do not reach the outlandish proportions of the wealthy in the United States; perhaps one reason is that Chileans are repelled by show-offs. But there are deeper reasons—reasons that evoke memories of the values of the conservative landowners themselves. For the North American drive for wealth is all but foreign to the Chilean. Accordingly, most Chileans have never developed much of what they could. Chilean waters abound in delicious sea foods, for example, but it is difficult to obtain a lobster in the country. Joseph Fichter once complained to me: "Eight million people, 2500 miles of shoreline, and it costs you five or six dollars for a lobster in a good Santiago hotel. I could never get over that."

Private investment in Chile runs to less than 5 percent of the country's Gross National Product. Nor historically has the Chilean invested his intellectual resources in his own country. Many of the best talents are found not in Chile developing the country, but managing international agencies and serving on various global committees.

Whenever he can, the educated, even moderately wealthy Chilean travels abroad, where he makes his purchases, thereby avoiding lofty Chilean sales taxes. The upper classes have always been subject to low rates of income taxes (a net rate of 15 percent on taxable income would be a high figure) and they have been extremely lax in paying. Where prosecution has resulted, the strategy has been to secure postponement; when the penalty is finally paid, the moneys are worth only about one-tenth of the amount assessed at the time the infraction was committed. "One of the effects of this gentle policy," reports sociologist George M. Korb, "is to prevent the accumulation of social capital in the form of education, roads and other public works. Thus, we find that neither the government nor those with wealth are providing an economic base for social mobility."

Why this lack of genuine concern for change? Korb, who studied Chilean society for two years, suggests one possible answer:

Within his own character, the Chilean has a great obstacle to material advancement. He does not admire the self-reliance, practicality and competitiveness that are so valued in our country, but considers kinship ties and affective personal relations as the worthwhile things of life. Almsgiving and sharing are deeply ingrained in his culture, and lack of generosity is held to be a grievous personal defect. You may compliment a person who works hard for being *trabajador*, a good worker, but to call him *ambicioso* is to imply that he is working for his own selfish ends. Social mobility is throttled when one may not excel others in his group, or when, if he does, he must support them. Most will not try. The lack of ambition of which North Americans complain is a deliberate choice.

The contentment of well-to-do Chileans with their lives expresses itself in wry, at times explosive, humor about others. "They have a low opinion of just about everybody," John Elac observes. "The Peruvians are square, the Bolivians are Indians, the Brazilians are too fun-loving." The greatest contempt is reserved for a favorite Latin American target, the Argentines. Chileans find them pompous. One Chilean comedian produces boisterous laughter with his routine about an international airport. It begins as Bolivian Airlines announces the departure of Flight # 001 and ends as Argentine Airlines announces the departure of Flight # 8,842,472.

The Chileans themselves are mostly a homogeneous people of Spanish-Caucasian stock, with some Araucanian Indian influence. European immigration over the last century has been small but decisive, with many English, Germans, Italians and lately Lebanese taking important roles in commercial society. The Germans settled mainly in the South, particularly around Valdivia, Osorno and Puerto Varas. There they prospered by carefully and thoroughly developing the land. The French and English went into mining. Arabs and Jews thrived in banking and textiles. "You go to a small town," notes a Chilean, "and who owns the exchange? Arabs."

First-generation immigrants remained as separate from

Chileans as they have traditionally from nationals in other countries. They formed their own clubs, banks and commercial societies. But national origins broke down quickly in the second generation, and the Spanish-speaking offspring of the immigrants were absorbed into Chilean life. There is prejudice in Chile, but it is less common and of a milder variety than in the United States. The Chileans make jokes about the way Arabs speak Spanish, or about Jews and their money, but the banter is more often good-natured than malicious. "If tomorrow an Arab makes a big crime, there is not going to be prejudice against the Arabs," a Chilean boasts. Most clubs today have Jewish members. Outright discrimination still exists, however, in the highest Chilean social circles. Recently a member of Los Leones, the best Santiago country club, suggested that an applicant shouldn't be admitted because he was Jewish. The man found out about it and did what Jews have done in response throughout the world. He formed his own club.

Whatever rejection of Jews and others exists within Chilean society today is often not founded on objection to origins, but to the manner in which the outsider made his money. For aristocracy in Chile is based on land ownership. To say that a man "made his money in business" is a way of degrading him. Such a man is not accepted by the elite, no matter how wealthy he may be. A man whose family owns land is accepted, no matter how destitute he may be.

Chilean life is totally fragmented on a class basis. "When the *chileno* doesn't know who you are, he makes no attempt at courtesy," says a veteran observer of Chilean life. "When he knows you, or thinks you're of a higher class, he falls all over himself."

A Chilean woman will dedicate herself to public service,

but until recently she wouldn't be seen at tea with a woman beneath her socially. At parties, groups would disperse into different corners, along class lines. A man who marries beneath his class invites not only social but commercial and political difficulties as well. "Chile is so small that if you trespass in any way, life can be miserable," says novelist José Donoso, whose recent book, *Coronación*, was a devastating portrayal of archaic Chilean society. "If you get on the good books of the *Mercurio* critic, you sell. If not, you're dead. He thinks Guy de Maupassant is a great innovator."

The Chilean upper-middle class is the group in Latin America most like the French bourgeoisie. Its interests (and the means taken to protect them) inhibit change almost as significantly as do the interests of the elite. For example, the Chilean labor code is supposed to be the most democratic in the hemisphere. Close inspection, however, reveals that it is designed to maintain a rigid set of values. White- and blue-collar workers must be represented by different unions; they are not permitted the same agreement; they have—by law—different minimum wages, family allowances, social security, termination benefits. All favor the white-collar worker. When Chilean crane operators organized to obtain certain white-collar benefits, a law was passed stipulating that they were *empleados* (employees) and not *obreros* (workers). Changing class is a legislative matter.

"According to Article 10 of its Constitution," George Korb wrote in *America*, a North American Jesuit weekly, "Chile has no privileged classes. Yet in this country, the most ignorant man on the street can distinguish three classes: *patrón*, *empleado* and *obrero*. . . . The minimum-wage law distinguishes two categories of labor: the *em-*

pleados and the *obreros*. They are roughly equivalent to nonmanual and manual labor. Last year [in 1961] the minimum wage of an *empleado* was about $64 a month, while the *obrero* received about $30. This means that a teen-age girl recently graduated from high school would earn more than twice as much as an adult laboring man with a family to support."

Social security benefits highlight the different values given to men by Chilean society. The ratio of benefits are in the same 2 to 1 ratio as salaries, white-collar workers receiving four times as much per dependent as do blue-collar workers. Says Korb: "This implies that a middle-class child deserves and needs, of the things money will buy, four times as much as a working-class child. It also indicates that in privilege-less Chile some people are even less privileged than others."

It is in education that the gap between ideal and real democracy widens most perceptibly.

The sophistication and intellectual veneer of the educated young Chilean might well dazzle his North American counterpart. The Chilean's English would probably be superior to the American's Spanish. His cultural base would be more profound. He would be more attuned to the social and economic dynamics of his own country. He would, in all probability, be more worldly. Yet the system that educated him must be called a failure. Auxiliary Bishop Mark G. McGrath, who lived in Chile for a number of years, once wrote: "It is impossible to compare the Chilean high school students with their counterparts in the United States without previously making it quite clear how few Chilean boys ever reach high school. . . ."

The statistics tell their own grim story. Of a hundred Chilean children, eleven never enter school. Of the eighty-nine who do, only twenty-five finish their primary education. Of these twenty-five, six enter vocational schools, but only three of the six stay three years or more; twelve of the twenty-five enter secondary school, but only three finish. Of those three, one begins work with a general education but no real skills. Two enter a university. Of these two, one finishes.

For Chile the effect is devastating. In 1962 roughly 13 percent of primary school-age children were not in school; 78 percent of secondary school-age children were not getting an education; 98 percent of university-age persons had fallen by the wayside.

Whether intentionally or inadvertently, the Chilean educational system greatly favors the wealthy over the poor. In Santiago, according to Korb, only 14 percent of children from poor families reach the first year of secondary school, compared to 32 percent of middle-income and 73 percent of upper-income children. In the private schools, the wealthy tend to perpetuate themselves. It is the custom of these schools to give scholarships to students from families with more than three children in the school. "Once again, the principle of 'he who has, gets' applies," notes Korb. "Instead of granting scholarships to needy students of outstanding ability, the schools' criterion is simply relationship with those already inside the charmed circle, without regard for personal ability or achievement."

Given the obstacles they encounter, the 99 percent of young Chileans who never had a chance of gaining a university education find no satisfaction in knowing that it is free. Theirs is not simply a loss of opportunity; it is a psychological defeat. Three American experts who went to Chile in 1964 to review man power and educational planning for the Chile-California Program (a project begun late in 1963 by President Kennedy with the hope that other states would form similar relationships with other Latin American countries, and financed by the U.S. and Chilean governments), concluded laconically: ". . . much of Chile's education system, and, in fact, man-power institutions, seems to be inadvertently designed to produce failures, not successes. . . . Of a hundred who start primary school, only the one who completes university is considered a success. The system and the society implicitly tend to make the ninety-nine who either drop our or are screened out along the way consider themselves failures."

The first eight years of a child's academic life may determine his fate. If by the end of that period he is not judged to be capable, he may be dropped from school, since scarce Chilean resources as a rule must be reserved for those who show more promise.

Since 1961 I have watched one little Chilean girl battling through these critical years. Her name is Olga Bravo. She was six when I first knew her; she would be seven, she told me "when I am grown up." When Olga plays she can be bright, intense and impish. But there was little spark to her the day I met her; rather, she was solemn, subdued and frightened.

She had come with her mother to a three-room schoolhouse on the edge of a dirt road in a small grape-growing town about fifty kilometers from Santiago. It was registration day. As Olga's mother sat at a desk to inscribe her daughter's name, Olga pushed next to her. In the dim light of the room her enormous eyes stood out.

Once Olga was enrolled her mother took her outside. Together they watched a dozen young girls and boys playing in the yard. Olga's mother pushed her daughter from her and told her to play. But Olga would not join in. Instead, she drifted over to the flagpole, and leaning against it, watched. She seemed so hopelessly burdened for a six-year-old. Talking to her mother I found out why.

A few months earlier Olga had reached school age. But the school nearest their house was five kilometers away. Since she was too young to travel alone her mother would have had to take her to school, fetch her for lunch, take her back and finally call for her at day's end. There was the problem of Olga's younger sister and brother. There was the problem of her mother's time. And there was, most of all, the problem of money. Bus fares, even with student rates, would add up to a sum the Bravos simply didn't have.

Felix Bravo is a slight, quiet, handsome man. He is illiterate. So is Olga's mother, Mercedes. So are all the members of both families. Felix Bravo learned to sign his name by copying a sample over and over. Mercedes Bravo was removed from school after two months to care for her brothers. Both Felix and Mercedes vowed that Olga should not live as they did, in one room of a house shared by five families, on $20 a month and sometimes, when there was no work, on nothing. "The girl must learn to read and write. It is not possible that she should be like us," her father said.

Early that year the parents decided that Olga must go to live with her godmother, whose house was across the street from a new school in a village twenty miles away. When Olga heard their decision she was happy. "I want to study," she said. Two weeks before registration she moved so that she would become accustomed to the separation from her parents, her sister and brother.

At first she was brave, but later she cried. One night she told her godmother that her mother had forgotten to bring her doll and she would have to go home.

As the week progressed Olga made friends with her godmother's duck, and things were a little better. On Sunday, the day before school, Olga's family came to visit. Olga was almost uncontrollably gay. She showed her books to her father and tried to copy some letters for him. She chased the duck and swung from a tree. At one point she took her father's handkerchief, and twirling it about her head, danced the *cueca*. But when the family rose to go Olga burst into tears.

By the next morning, however, excitement had conquered sorrow. Olga rose at dawn, put on her white student's uniform and prepared her books. An hour before school was to begin she heard a bus stop in the street, and she looked outside. "Teacher's here," she cried, and with the other children from nearby homes raced to the school. That day she learned to pull her chair in and out quietly. She drew flowers and played games. And she decided to become a schoolteacher.

At the time it seemed conceivable. A few months later I received a report from Olga's teacher. Olga was attentive. She was learning to read and write. Her teacher thought surely that Olga had some kind of academic future.

But at some point after the teacher reported, the pressure of separation began to affect Olga. Her attention wavered; her work fell off. Slowly, she began to slip behind. By the time Olga's parents moved her home in 1963 Olga was already doing poorly.

The Bravos put Olga into an impoverished Catholic school monitored by aged nuns. The nuns put Olga back a year. She quickly became the butt of the jokes of children her age. She took their kidding gamely—as she did the sarcasm of the nuns.

Late in 1964 Felix and Mercedes Bravo separated. Mercedes soon began to live with another man. Olga moved to a *callampa* in Santiago where she is now living with an aunt.

Soon her formal education will end. It isn't too difficult to predict what will happen to her then. By the harsh standards of slum-dwelling life she will be big enough and old enough to make her own bid to struggle out. The easiest, most apparent route will be that of a domestic. She will move then, if she's lucky, to the Barrio Alto, where she will begin to work a fifteen-hour day at the lowest domestic's salary. Because she is pretty she will begin to see boys when she is about fifteen. If she is very fortunate, she will marry a devoted man when she is seventeen or eighteen, and thereby make her escape. But the odds against that are enormous. Devotion among Chilean lower-class men is not customarily constant or prolonged. In any event, her man might take her right back to the slums.

I have dwelt on the story of Olga at length because she is my friend, but also because I wanted to humanize the ciphers of Chilean poverty. If the Chilean educational system were democratic, there would be resources for Olga Bravo and thousands of other girls and boys like her. In all Chile there are scarcely a hundred guidance or educational counselors working in the schools. More to the point, if the Chilean educational system were to reflect the Chilean reality, it would be designed for the student who has no chance or intention of going into higher education, as well as providing for the student with scholastic potential. The survey of man power and educational needs made by U.S. experts showed that "this principle appears to be ignored right in the mainstream of Chile's secondary education. Everything . . . is pointed toward university, yet even of those hardy few (in relative terms) who complete *secundaria*, only one in three, or less, will successfully make it into the second year of university. The present arrangement is to brand all students who do not go on as failures and to give them little or no basis for finding useful employment. Eventually most of them do find employment. . . . But in the process there is much unnecessary personal frustration, if not tragedy."

The tragedy is not simply personal; it is national. By depriving the majority of Chilean youth of educational opportunity, Chile deprives itself of the power to move ahead. "The economy needs, and will continue to need, large numbers of such middle-level man power," the U.S. analysis says. ". . . They need only possess a good general education, have the flexibility for quick on-the-job training and retraining, and some attitude and discipline for productive employment. The *secundaria* school could do more to give these attributes if it set about to do so and abandoned the fiction that it is solely a university preparatory system."

The study emphasized the striking capacity of the Chilean labor force, its sophistication, its energy, its willingness. Its neglect, therefore, seems all the more tragic.

The lack of educational opportunity extends into the industrial-vocational area as well. While the situation has improved considerably in recent years, historically, few Chilean industrialists have understood the value of training their workers to produce better. Korb tells the story of the U.S. Point Four engineer who recommended to one industrialist that he set up a training program for his workers, in order to increase their obviously deficient productivity. The industrialist rejected the idea. Once the men were trained, he said, they would go elsewhere for more money. "But if they produce more, you can meet the wage scale of any of your competitors," the Point Four engineer argued. The Chilean couldn't see it. Today, many sons of Chilean immigrants train their workers; most Chileans of traditional stock do not.

Productivity increases basically for two reasons: an increase in capital investment and an improvement in technology and worker education and training. Of the two factors, the second is at least five times as important as the first. But in Chile, not only do industrialists fail to invest their financial capital, they fail to invest in human capital, as well. They are not aware that education is an investment.

Thus we find in Chile a phenomenon that feeds on itself. Members of the Chilean elite study primarily in law, the humanities and social services, leaving Chile with a chronic shortage of engineers, physicians, dentists, architects, agronomists, and other technical people. The shortage, coupled with—or indeed caused by—the lassitude of Chile's business leaders, creates its own lassitude in the Chilean economy. Talented, trained Chileans, lacking local opportunity, go abroad to employ their skills fully. The irony of this situation was described in 1964 by Sergio Gutiérrez-Olivos, then Chile's ambassador to the United States, in an address at Portland University in Oregon:

Chile has been able to produce, at considerable sacrifice, a group of scientists, professional men, economists and technicians who meet high standards. At the present intermediate stage of its development, Chile's access to this elite group is like having access to a necessary and invaluable treasure that is always in danger of slipping away. It is paradoxical that this danger should lie precisely in the training that the country has given this group, because this training explains the unsatisfied ambitions and readiness of the group to seize opportunities open to it abroad. . . . I can cite, for example, the perhaps unusual but by no means unique situation where Chilean experts are called upon to serve in international organizations, while technical assistance missions are sent to Chile to perform the tasks that should properly be theirs.

We must now seek answers to some puzzling questions. *Why* do Chilean industrialists not have more verve? *Why* is the society, as a whole, not more ambitious? *Why* is the educational system structured for the elite? *Why* is Chilean life structured so rigidly along class lines? And, finally, *why* does this society, which calls itself democratic, fail to make real the idea of equality?

If these questions can be answered, we might then understand not simply the Chilean dilemma but the dilemma of Latin America.

The Timid Giant

Certainly neither man nor any of his institutions can be blamed exclusively for his failures. National backwardness can be traced frequently to a debilitating climate, meagre resources or a series of natural misfortunes. Neither of the first two reasons applies to Chile. In the productive central area the climate is inspiring, neither hot nor cold, mostly fresh and pleasant. Chile has yet to exploit fully the copper, nitrates, coal, oil and ore beneath her land —or the land itself. Yet several important geographic factors do apply to Chile.

The first is the country's outlandish shape. From an economic point of view most countries are organized in circles. Chile is a strip. Her cities cannot engage in commerce with wide, encircling areas; they must nourish, instead, on the lands directly above and below them. This limits markets, raises transportation costs and brakes expansion.

A second geographic factor is distance. Chile is far from the developed centers of the world. A soaring mountain range separates her from the nearest center, Argentina.

Her ships must plow thousands of miles to foreign ports. As a result, her trading volume has been scant by comparison with trading norms.

But the major natural cause of frustrated development has been a tragic joust with the elements. One hundred and thirty-five times since the Spanish conquest, thirty times in the twentieth century alone, tremors have shaken Chile, most often slightly, but on occasion with devastating effect. In 1906 an earthquake destroyed the port city of Valparaíso. The earthquake of 1928 destroyed Talca. The earthquake of 1939 killed 20,000 persons of a country then numbering five million—proportionally more persons than the United States lost in World War II. The earthquake of 1960 required an expenditure of 10 percent of the national capital to rehabilitate the country. The earthquake of 1965 cost $400 million—half of Chile's net investment for that year. "This country," says Chile's illustrious economist, Raúl Sáez, "is fighting very difficult conditions."

Yet, ultimately, backwardness is caused by man.

It is often said that the difference between North America and Latin America can be explained by the reasons each was settled. Our people, borne on waves of persecution came to the New World to stay. They brought their families and their possessions; they never thought of returning to Europe; rather, they dug in to prosper. But the Iberians who roamed Latin America came chiefly in search of treasures so they could build estates for their waiting families in Spain and Portugal. Initially there was no thought of remaining in the New World. Nor was there planning or progress.

There were other obvious reasons why our patterns diverged. The United States almost always had more capital than man power, a stimulating proportion for economic growth. Chile, like the rest of Latin America, has always had more man power than capital, a situation that requires a large investment in unproductive services. The United States has several times gone to war, a process that inevitably arouses an economy; Chile warred actively only three times in her history, from 1836 to 1839 against the Peru-Bolivia confederation, in 1866 when she declared war against Spain, and from 1879 to 1883 in the War of the Pacific. Nothing of a sustained nature has ever "pushed" the Chileans since—no emergency, no threat, no Protestant Ethic. "We were a more traditional, rural society," observes Renato Poblete, a Chilean Jesuit sociologist. "Economic conditions created a mentality of acceptance. On the farm, the *hacendado* had better candlelight than the worker, but they both had candlelight. The *hacendado* had a better horse, but they both rode to town on a horse. For mobility of people, you have to create tension and aspiration. We had no historical events to do that until the tension imposed by technology." Technology did not change reality for the poor people of Chile, but it did widen the gap between reality and aspiration. Says Father Poblete: "Aspiration is the great motor for social change."

In psychological terms, it can be said that a society's actions are the projection of a collective will or ideal. In Latin America this "social superego" simply does not exist. While Latin Americans are as generous and charitable as any other group, they have, until recent years, failed to understand that the individual has responsibilities to society. The Latin American covets the privileges of democracy, but he rarely perceives its obligations. A young priest I know expressed the result very simply: "They give things

—but they don't do reforms in their own places." To illustrate he took me to see the workers' quarters on a hacienda that belonged to a charitable Catholic family. "There," he said, pointing. Against the hillside I could see a neat row of whitewashed buildings that seemed, if not lavish, at least adequate. "You mean those?" I asked in surprise. "No, those are for horses," he explained. "The others are for men." I looked more closely. Against the hillside were the workers' shacks, sagging, barren, so drab they blended with the dirt.

In his report, *Latin-American Catholicism: A Self-Evaluation*, Father William J. Coleman observes: "Society possessed an informal social relief and welfare agency, directed by charitable people of means who looked after known cases of exceptional need and of misery. But at the same time there was in this society a complete ignorance of, and almost an invincible failure to notice, endemic and generalized conditions of poverty and misery."

What kind of mentality can embrace both enormous charity and social indifference? It is the mentality of a man who perceives his own, his family's and his friends' situation acutely, who neglects the needs of society not through selfishness or some other whim, but simply because he is constitutionally incapable of seeing the world around him, who thinks not of the public good, but of what is good for him.

The great handicap of the Latin American is his inheritance—an embracing set of Hispanic values.

Hispanism [writes Fredrick Pike] places dignity, status and manners above talent and tangible accomplishments, the supernatural graces believed to flow from the Catholic faith above deeds that produce good results on the mundane level, dogma above curiosity, authoritarianism above democracy, family above communal good, permanent, stratified order in the social structure above flux, and resignation to the physical ambient above endeavors to reform and improve it. Hispanism also honors the traditional more than the new, and the graceful and artistic more than the functional and the practical. Finally, as the name implies, Hispanism entails veneration of Spain and Spanish civilization as the foundation of virtue, morality and culture, and as the vital source of all that is good in the New World.

The *conquistadores* who came to the New World branded the land. They were Iberians, fiercely individualistic men, concerned principally with the freedom to determine their own fate. In thirty years they conquered a continent, humbled a civilization, enslaved millions, melted golden works of art. They took land not for production, but for prestige; because they demeaned labor, they left it to their chattels. Some of the *conquistadores* were cynically realistic, but most convinced themselves that their actions were justified to Christianize the heathen.

Over the centuries, the disdain for work, the glorification of birth and property and the contempt for commerce and industry permeated the social marrow. When revolution swept Latin America in the early 1800's, its character was predetermined. The form of government might change, but social revolt was impossible. The young *criollos*, inspired by Jean-Jacques Rousseau's *Émile*, might write constitutions that exalted the rights of man and the democratic ideal, but the ideals could not be translated into reality. "They had tried futilely to establish in their countries forms of government in which liberty and democracy would thrive," writes Leopoldo Zea in *The Latin American Mind*. "The Hispanic Americans were not ready for either. The ideals of liberty and democracy on their lips were but words, simple pretexts, by which they sought their right to govern; that is, to impose their wills upon the wills of others. Each Hispanic American *caudillo* without regard for his mottoes or his banners, only aspired to occupy the place abandoned by the *conquistador*."

Why did no force emerge from this ferment to dominate the static tendencies of men? What motivates us? From where comes our hunger for success, excellence, justice, equality? We are seeing today in our racial struggles that such an ethos does not translate automatically into reality. It is made effective only by the force of our institutions—our government, civic groups, labor unions, religious and ethical organizations. Institutionally, we are a highly organized people.

What of Latin America? Its institutions are chaotically weak. Government has been historically more a reflection of the men who controlled it than of any all-encompassing national aspiration. Labor unions have demonstrated more political, than social and economic, effectiveness. Civic organizations, until recent years, did not exist. All that did exist—that has always existed—was the Roman Catholic Church.

"And do you swear that you will support the Conservative party?" asks the priest.

"I swear," says the sinner.

"And do you swear that you will never sell your vote?" the priest demands.

"I swear," says the sinner.

"And do you swear that if you do sell your vote, you will sell it to the Conservative party?"

"I swear," says the sinner.

(An old Chilean joke)

Nothing is so intricately woven into the fabric of Chilean—and Latin American—life and history as the Roman Catholic Church. Without an understanding of the role of the Church in the Southern Hemisphere, the Latin American problem itself cannot be comprehended. Yet no institution is currently so misunderstood.

North Americans (Catholics among them) believe that the Church in Latin America is wealthy, powerful, self-seeking, and as the anecdote above lightly suggests, allies itself with conservative elements to protect its position and possessions. While the image has a good deal of historical validity, it is hopelessly dated. Not only is the Church today unbelievably poor, it is, in crucial sectors of Latin American life, the single most aggressive force for democratic reform.

Its critics do not try the Church on the proper grounds. In religious terms, the Church can be charged with failure; as a social force it has been until recent years a timid giant.

Spiritually, the Church has all but failed in its mission to make what it would consider "good" Catholics out of the 90 percent of Latin Americans who say they are Catholics. The differences in religious practice between countries, and among economic groups within countries, are striking. "It ranges," notes a Jesuit sociologist, Joseph P. Fitzpatrick, "from an intensity of practice and devotion that is heroic, to an indifference that is difficult to conceive. But wherever it may be, the Catholicism of Latin America has characteristics of its own that generally baffle the outsider."

Most Latin American Catholics are ignorant of the fundamentals of their religion. They may profess certain beliefs, but they rarely employ them in daily life. If pressed, they will deny that the pope is infallible or that Hell exists. Among the lower classes, marriage is rarely formalized. Among the upper classes divorce is, of course, unknown, but the effect is achieved through annulment, which is fre-

quently granted on the grounds that the partners were not
married in their home parish. (Marriage ceremonies, con-
sequently, are often prudently arranged for a neutral parish.) A panoramic view of Latin American Catholicism by
Father Coleman, a Maryknoll priest, well describes Chile:

> . . . together with the deepest Catholic piety and devotion
> to the Blessed Virgin [one finds] no real regard for the Mass
> and the sacraments. An almost fanatical concern for the
> Sacrament of Baptism, . . . is joined to a profoundly cynical
> view of the Sacrament of Matrimony. . . . . Whatever may
> be the tradition of this Catholicism, it reflects no real grasp
> of fundamental Catholic principles and suppositions.

North American Catholics will find the specifics of Chilean religious life developed by the Jesuit sociologist
Renato Poblete barely credible. Between 85 and 90 percent of Chile's 8,500,000 people are baptized. Yet each
Sunday, only 800,000 go to Mass. In the north of Chile,
attendance at Sunday Mass is estimated at between 4 to 10
percent of the population; in the center, between 16 and 25
percent; in the south, less than 10 percent. In some Santiago slums practice drops lower than 1 percent. The oldest
are the most religious, the youngest the least religious.
Above the age of sixty, between 7.6 and 20 percent of the
men observe; among women, between 14.4 and 36.5 percent. But in the twenty-first to thirty age-group, only 3
percent of the men, and between 5.6 percent and 19 percent of the women practice, depending on the region.

An insight into why so few Latin American men attend
Church is found in an incident described by Monsignor
Luigi Ligutti, one of the Vatican's most effective Latin
American observers.

> I knew a priest once who told me that his mother had a
> large piece of property with a huge old house on it. She had

decided that she wanted to give it to some missionary order, and he asked my advice as to what orders to consider. I told him of an order of women in the U.S. who would work out very well. He said, "No, the Church is already too feminine in Latin America." This was a very significant remark. A large percentage of the men in Latin America who are Catholics do not go to Church. They don't want to be considered "pious duds." It is all right for women to be devout, but somehow it is not virile for a man.

A paucity of priests also accounts for the indifference of many Catholics. There was but one priest for every 3000 Catholics in Chile in 1960, compared to one for every 700 in North America. Among rural populations the ratio is much higher; in such areas, the people may see a priest only once every six months. If and when they move to the city, the habit of vague observance continues.

The consequences of the Church's lack of penetration are shown in a study made among Chilean urban workers by Father John Considine:

> Of fifty-six marriages studied, in only two cases could it be established that the unions came about through elevated Christian motives. In thirty-four cases, . . . they represented for the worker a combination of sex motives and a general friendly inclination toward the woman. In twenty cases, . . . the union was entered into solely for physical sex reasons with no love element evident. . . . Abortion was well known and favored by 60 percent of the men queried. . . . There were very few unmarried mothers because the opinion was current in the area that no soul was present until four months after conception and thus no great moral harm was involved in early abortion. . . .

One surveyor reported: "It is completely clear and evident that the Church does not reach the worker. . . . The priest. . . . is eyed with suspicion . . . all that he stands for is regarded

70

as false and given no consideration. . . ." Said another surveyor: "The worker has no inclination to participate in this organization that he regards as being managed completely by . . . the rich."

Catholicism follows much the same pattern throughout Latin America. The average Catholic tends to be casual in practice, indifferent to religious requirements, yet deeply emotional about his "commitment." A Maryknoll father in Lima told me about a man who would repeatedly insist, *"Soy muy católico,* I am very Catholic." Said the priest: "He's got four wives in different cities—but he always blesses himself when he passes a church."

In Catholic terms, therefore, much of Latin America is still "missionary country." But the failure of the Catholic Church goes much deeper. It goes to the core of the Latin American failure itself—the abysmal state of its social structures.

The history of the Church in Latin America shines with examples of the humaneness of many priests. Many priests pleaded against maltreatment of the Indians and fought against slavery; some even led rebellions of the oppressed. At each critical moment in Latin American history, a small progressive group has led the Church to higher ground. But these priests have almost always emphasized charity, almost never responsibility. "I'm from a rich family," a young Peruvian priest once told me. "I can say I've never heard about social responsibility from that source in my life. Never. And my family is a very Christian family. We were surrounded by priests." When German priests with whom the young man came in contact told him about the social doctrine of the Church, "it was a revelation."

Spanish Catholicism has never been incarnational—it has never concerned itself with man's life in this world—but has concentrated, instead, on preparation for the after-life. Because the Church was passive about social responsibility, it gave no inspiration to the individual Catholic. Lacking a model—either from family or Church (which should have given it to family)—the individual did not develop a sense of social obligation. And since there were no other inspirational forces on which the individual could base an idea of conduct, the ideal never developed. The Hispanic values of family, individualism, status, dogma, rigidity and resignation smothered the revolutionary ideas of country, endeavor, duty, service, flexibility and change.

The effect has been devastating—little material progress, an inability to believe in mankind. For example, graduates of Catholic universities in Chile "do not have faith in human beings," Joseph Fichter, the Jesuit sociologist, concluded after a study several years ago.

> They do not have confidence in the common man. They do not believe that farm laborers can be trained in successful farming methods. They do not believe that the sons of workers could succeed as university students. In other words, the kind and amount of education that these university graduates have had did not instill in them one of the most important and cherished values of a Christian and democratic society: the belief that abilities and the opportunity to use these abilities are not exclusively the possession of one class, or race, or type of family.

The need for the Church to admonish its adherents is particularly crucial because of the static characteristics of the faith—a fact that leaders in the Church's current social-reform drive persistently point out. Says Auxiliary Bishop McGrath: "Many Catholics, wedded to an exaggerated

72

fixity in all matters concerning the teaching and the practice of the Church, unconsciously project this attitude into an opposition towards, or at least a suspicion of, all change in the social realm." The Belgian-born Jesuit, Roger Vekemans, is even more emphatic:

> The sacred and profane worlds should be kept apart. In the sacred world, I'm a typically obedient man. I believe in God because that's that. The priest tells me there is Heaven and I believe that because he is a representative of God. That's gospel. But this interpersonal relationship is irrelevant in the profane world. Outside the sacred world, I would never obey one man. For us, everything has been said through the last apostle. This tradition, when you bring it into the profane world, is of course, a barrier. The profane world is in evolution. In the profane world, I have to discover. It hasn't been revealed to me.

A dogmatic Catholic, lacking any social consciousness, content with life as it was, created the political, economic and social problems that Latin America faces today. "The blame?" Father Vekemans asks rhetorically:

> To the Church as a mystical body, not at all. To the Church as a social body, of course. It's an unconscious fault, not a deliberate one. It's not the guilt of the religious society, but it is a guilt to be held *against* the religious society. An offense against the profane world is a sin against the religious society.
>
> An overly spiritualized religion can exist without challenge in a static society, which Latin America was for several centuries. But when it comes in contact with the harsh realities of a headlong society, a conflict arises. People see that the Church has been here for four centuries and doesn't seem able to make for them a life they can be satisfied with in the face of modern advances.

It is to that precise challenge that the Church is responding today—and nowhere more so than in Chile.

Why did the Catholic Church not advance its ample social doctrine in Latin America until recent years? This question produces an almost reflex response: the Church wished to protect its own considerable wealth. Few ideas about Latin America are so current, and few are so worthless.

Historically, the relationship between the clergy and the upper class has been powerful and palpable. Where the clergyman himself came from the upper class (as did so many bishops), he brought to his office an upper-class mentality. Educated priests had a great intellectual bond with other educated men, most of whom were conservative. Through the years the Church maintained a close political relationship with the conservative classes. But the reasons usually given to explain the connection are largely contrary to the truth. For the "wealthy" Catholic Church in Latin America is a pauper, beholden to those who give her alms.

It is widely assumed that the Church uniformly dominates Latin American life. The reality, however, must include an articulate and influential minority that criticizes and rejects the Church on intellectual grounds, and a much larger group, that although nominally Catholic, is bitterly anti-clerical. In Colombia the rag ends of a hundred-year-old civil war over the role of the Church in society still wave. In Mexico and Uruguay priests are not permitted to wear clerical garb in the streets. A too-loud mention of the Church provokes a sudden, menacing glance.

Such feelings are political hangovers that have lasted for 150 years. When Spain conquered the New World, it installed a Church that it, not Rome, controlled. Thus, when the Latin Americans overthrew Spanish rule in the early 1800's, they were also overthrowing the Spanish-Catholic

Church. In most instances the new nations seized the properties of the Church. The Church has never recovered.

The properties of the Church, which before the revolutionary period were so immense as to defy calculation, had been bequeathed by wealthy Catholics. Income from the properties had been used to finance Church works, and more importantly, to sustain the Church itself. Today such income is generally so meagre that most dioceses would quickly cease to function without additional help.

Such a portrait stands seemingly in contrast to what the eye can see—gold-gilded churches laden with treasures. It must be remembered that most of these churches were constructed hundreds of years ago, many by the *conquistadores*, and that aside from the land they stand on they have little or no commercial value today. As one priest put it: "There are no buyers for churches."

"What should we do, sell the churches and give the money to the people?" asks Monsignor Ligutti. "How long do you think it would last? Not a month, not a week, and then there would be nothing. In 1953 I put ads in *Christian Century* and some other publications asking anyone with information about the landed interest of the Church in Latin America to come to me and show it to me. This was not done facetiously. I meant it, but no one ever answered that ad. The Church just doesn't have a great deal of income property or landed interest in Latin America."

In 1962 I spent several months investigating the financial situation of the Church in Colombia, Peru and Chile. In some cases, to my surprise, Church officials happily volunteered figures. In other cases the information came from a scrutiny of property roles, block by block, region by region, with the surreptitious help of government officials and others. At the end of this research, I could only conclude that if the three examples studied were typical, the Church in Latin America today is very poor, indeed.

Perhaps the closest the image of the wealthy Church comes to accuracy is in Colombia, where the Church owns roughly 2.5 percent of the country's urban and rural real estate, worth an estimated $100 million. But an American banker, after completing a study the Church had requested, recommended that the holdings be liquidated since they were unproductive. The money, he said, should be invested in people, who, better trained, better cared for, would support the Church in return.

A more realistic idea of the financial situation of the Church in Colombia is provided by that of its major archdiocese, Bogotá. Until recently, when it was divided, the archdiocese had 2,000,000 persons. But its working capital was—and is—$30,000. It has no income-producing property; only one of its 110 parishes does. The sole building the archdiocese owns is the palace in which it is headquartered—a gift from the government in 1948. Msgr. Ernesto Umaña, who directs the financial affairs of the archdiocese, only half in jest told me, "I would be very happy to sell the palace and invest the money in other things."

In Lima the Church owns roughly 1 percent of urban commercial property, according to official statistics. But the benefits of these properties are circumscribed by frozen rentals, regulations prohibiting eviction of tenants (and thereby, redevelopment), severe conditions imposed by donors, and finally, the inability of the Church to sell without Vatican approval. Notes a city planner: "In spite of being a very large property owner, the Church would be rich only if and when she could sell all or part of that property. From the rent she receives, she is a very poor person."

In many countries the big property owners within the

Church are the religious orders. But the properties usually are not well run, and the yield from them is low.

In Chile the Catholic Church owns less than 1 percent of the lands. The dioceses are universally poor.

The Archdiocese of Santiago, which serves 2,250,000 Catholics has a yearly income of about $165,000. Three-fourths of this amount comes from donations. The other quarter comes from property rentals—but nearly half of this sum is lost to the Church, since it is putting the lands under agrarian reform.

The Diocese of Temuco receives $2000 a year, mostly from a foundation set up in its behalf. Its bishop, Bernardino Piñera, receives $50 a month in addition to his food and lodgings. The Diocese of Talca, whose bishop, Manuel Larraín, is a leader in the Church's Latin American reform movement, has an income of $13,750 a year; its expenses are twice that amount (largely because it runs thirty-two free schools) and must be made up by donations. The bishop's salary is $40 a month.

What happens when the Church cannot support itself? A study by a Chilean Jesuit, Mario Zañartu, gives some clues: "There are only two ways of financing left to it, either to appeal to the generous among the wealthy or to charge for services. Both systems, however, lead to the same slavery—dependence on the wealthy classes." Laments one young priest: "Unless the Church is supported, the priest can't live."

It was a poor, vulnerable Church that had to pick its way through the post-revolutionary nineteenth-century secular world of Latin America. The cost was high. Recalls Emilio Maspero, a labor leader:

> In the face of the image of the Church's historic compromises with money, power, and privilege, the working masses developed a hostility, not only to the unjust economic and

social institutions, but also to the Church, which in their eyes has been systematically and relentlessly supporting the established order, and unjust and inhuman social and economic institutions. This has stirred a deep-seated anti-clericalism, drawing the masses away from faith in Christianity and pushing them toward faith in Communism. . . .

By 1915 it was clear to some Chilean priests that if the Church were to continue in this manner, it might one day be overwhelmed. At the risk of offending the very people who fed them, these priests began to preach the social doctrine that had first been expressed in 1891 in the papal encyclical, *Rerum Novarum* and would be amplified by *Quadragesimo Anno*. But their efforts met with rebuff from the upper classes as well as conservative priests. One veteran of that struggle remembers the reaction of the aristocracy when the second encyclical was promulgated in 1931: " 'This is very pretty,' they said, 'but it has no application to Chile. We must assist the poor, we must seek to alleviate their suffering, but the poor will always be poor. Our Father has said that they always will be, and so it will do no good to change the social structure. We are Catholic countries. Nothing will happen.' It was a type of false peace."

For several weeks, representatives of the Archbishop attempted to convince the Conservative party newspaper, *El Diario Illustrado*, to publish the new encyclical. They failed. An editor told them, "It is necessary to protect the Catholics from the imprudences of the Pope."

It was during these early struggles that two liberal priests, Fernando Vives and Jorge Fernández Pradel, suffered what one historian describes as "a lack of understanding with the upper classes," and Conservative influence prevailed on the Church to pack them off to Europe so that a peaceful relationship could be maintained. But by

1932 both were back. With several colleagues they proceeded to animate an extraordinary group of twenty precocious, intense, young Chilean-Catholics. One of the twenty, their leader, was a brilliant student named Eduardo Frei Montalva.

4

"He Does Not Have the Face of a Happy Man"

He was poor, the son of an immigrant Swiss-Protestant father and a Chilean-Catholic mother. A friend remembers him in the patio of their high school one winter day, wearing summer clothes, and without a coat. When he was sixteen his father fell ill, and for a while it appeared that Eduardo, the oldest of three children, would have to leave school to support the family. The idea appalled his father, who years before had left a good job as manager of a farm to return to Santiago and a low-paying job with the government so that his children could attend good schools. Eduardo's professors were equally appalled; he was their best student. Although there had been talk of a career in medicine, Eduardo instead studied law at the university; there he also taught several classes and continued to help support his family. His father died a few years after he received his law degree.

It was inevitable that by this time Eduardo was committed

to social problems. I once asked him why he, a poor man, had chosen to fight for society instead of himself. "It was instinctive," he responded. "It was due in part to the *ambiente* of my house. My father was not ambitious for money. I was always poor. When I was young I was very eager to read. I read a lot in the classics—about men, about the human condition. I always had an unrest, an inquietude. What responses could be given to the condition of man? I was preoccupied with social philosophy. The problem presented itself every day—the misery, the ideological battle we were going through. Since I was a child, I'd had a Christian formation. So this concern was natural."

And visible. He looked more serious than he should have, his thin face solemn, brow furrowed, eyes sweet but penetrating and heavy with thought. The look remains to this day. Says an admirer sadly: "He does not have the face of a happy man."

When he first came to Santiago he struck his new schoolmates as a hayseed. His dress was unfashionable; he seemed silent in contrast to those who had learned to match the city's turbulence with their own. Yet his classmates soon felt drawn to him. He was smarter than they. His voracious capacity for learning and love of books fascinated them. They liked to study next to him, because he would help them with problems they found too difficult.

He was a good athlete, not a star, but a sturdy playmaker in soccer, and a capable gymnast. He captained both teams, more because of his ability to mold and exhort them than for his own athletic power. He did not push his way into leadership; he did not have to. His teachers and fellow students would invite him to take charge. It would always be this way. "He has always had his own position and attitude," his friend of forty years, Javier Lagarrigue, observes. "He has never been a follower of others. He is convinced of his own ideas and strength." At some point early in his political life he began to develop a sense of calling. "He never said to me, 'I want to be president,'" Lagarrigue recalls, "but all those years we were always talking on the assumption that he was going to be president."

His drive amazed everyone, particularly his mother. With his work, athletics, and student activities, he would not get to his studies until late at night. He would finish early in the morning, sleep a few hours, and arise refreshed. An excellent listener and student, his face stern with concentration, he easily reached the top of his class, where he remained throughout his academic life. At his high-school graduation he gave the farewell address. In 1933 he graduated with the grand prize of Santiago's Catholic University awarded to the best student.

It was no mean feat. Eduardo was but one of a most unusual group of young Chilean men, perhaps the most brilliant ever to go through the university. All had great intellectual powers, all were puzzled by the Chile they were inheriting. They were dismayed and disappointed in their elders for having permitted dictatorship in Chile for the first time since the overthrow of Spain. As Eduardo Frei and his friends were finishing school the political life of the country was at a standstill.

Seen in perspective those years were a blessing. Instead of dissipating their energies on loud but meaningless political activities, the vibrant young men studied, and argued among themselves. Their liberal teacher-priests gave them books on Christian social philosophy. The message hit them hard. "They found it asked more than what they had been giving," recalls one of their teachers, Monsignor Jorge Gómez.

If the readings were illuminating for Frei, the contact with his brilliant friends was decisive. "We were all of the same social group, the same style of life," he recalls. "The middle class hated the upper class. We didn't. The middle class aspired to the figuration, the acceptance, the frivolity of the upper class. We didn't. We simply did not form part of the classic middle class."

The answer of the upper class to any threat from the middle class had always been absorption. But these young men were not to be absorbed. Instead in 1931 they organized the first Social Week in the history of Chile, an attempt to awaken the people to the country's social problems. By train, by horse, and when necessary, by foot, they fanned out into the provinces.

They found a desperate country, suffering from the backlash of the world-wide Depression. The price of copper, the country's main export, upon which it depended for dollars to buy vital imports, had fallen to six cents a pound. (It is 62 cents at this writing.) The Ibáñez government was becoming increasingly unpopular. Finally, on July 25, 1931, defiant students, refusing to knuckle under to the dictator, took command of the University of Chile. Ibáñez sent troops, but the students held. The next day Ibáñez left Chile, the troops retired and the students policed the country.

Chaos followed. In one period of 101 days, Chile had six governments. Generals traded power. Rebellious factions marched against one another in fruitless gestures. Frei and his friends watched the process with emptiness and dismay. It was a time for taking sides. Frei and his friends determined to enter politics. "The Marxists were responding to the social inequities and unrest," he says now. "We felt we had to offer our answer to the people."

Chile has always tolerated political difference. "In every good family, they feel disappointed if they don't have a son who is a Communist," one Chilean observes. Thus, in the thirties, many young men in Chile turned to socialism and communism. Frei had always argued with the Marxists. He had studied and written about Marxism, but it had never been an answer for him because of his Christian formation.

Much later he would reflect that

> The great mass of the people do not participate in the real life of the country. The democratic system has not been faithfully expressed. The fact that the privileged groups control the land, the banks and the journals has permitted the democratic system to conserve structures as they are. These groups can perpetuate the system by obtaining representation in Congress.

In 1933 Eduardo Frei, then twenty-two, left school with a degree in law, a following among other students, and a tested ability to organize. The following year he was offered an editor's job on a newspaper in the North. The region had always been considered left wing; there, the liberal viewpoint had been the province of Masonry and Radicalism, and most recently, of Marxism. Frei, then a member of the Conservative party, dreamed of mobilizing the party along the lines of the Church's modern social doctrine. He found the challenge irresistible and accepted the job.

Before leaving Santiago a friend warned him: "When you enter that newspaper office the walls and roof will collapse."

But Frei's editorship, while active, was uneventful—and his interest quickly moved to politics. In January 1937 he announced his candidacy as deputy for the area. To run his campaign, he summoned Radomiro Tomić from Santiago. Tomic, a fiery orator, more Left than Frei, was years later to be Frei's chief rival for the party leadership. Now, by car (often a battered taxi) and by truck, sometimes on foot, the twenty-six-year-old candidate and his twenty-two-year-old manager covered the district preaching national unity. But they were talking to embittered men, many of them Communists. Often they were drowned out by insults, and pelted with tomatoes and eggs. One evening, just as Frei was about to address a small crowd in a village square the lights went out, and he was hit by a hail of stones. He and Tomic were Catholics, identified with the most Catholic of parties, operating in an anti-Catholic area. "We were determined to make absolutely clear what Jesus said, 'To Caesar what belongs to Caesar, to God what belongs to God,' " Tomic recalls. But the task was impossible.

Frei lost the election. Afterward, in disgust, he announced that he was through with politics. He left the newspaper in Tomic's hands and returned to Santiago to become a professor of labor law at Catholic University. But it was soon evident that his mind was elsewhere. "He was a better professor of sociology than labor law," a former student recalls. "He was more interested in social ideas and fundamentals than the labor code. He was not a full-time dedicated professor to his subject. He was preoccupied with the basic issue involved, but not very much with legal techniques."

The following year Frei was back in politics, elected to lead the newly created movement of Conservative youth, the Falange Nacional. Events were beginning to develop that would shape the future of Chilean political life and cause Frei great personal anguish.

Chile had returned to civil government in 1932. Shortly

afterward, Conservative leaders, realizing that their own ranks had aged during the years of political activity, had approached the young men with an invitation to join their party. The group had split three ways over the issue. The first element thought that the Conservative party had nothing to say to the men of their day; the second was plainly Fascist, admired the Italians, and wanted a Fascist-style state for Chile; the third felt that they should join forces with the Conservative party anyway, in spite of its inadequacies, since it was the Catholic party. This they finally did, though opponents insisted to the last that the move would "break" their own "socio-economic" line.

From the outset the association was uneasy. It could not last. The rupture came in 1938 when the young men were asked to support the party's choice for president, Gustavo Ross. Instead, they put forward the names of five men acceptable to them. They were overruled, and Ross was nominated.

It was a tense time in the political life of Chile. An unpopular right-wing president, Arturo Alessandri Palma, was leaving office. A ragtag coalition, representing all groups from aristocrat to communist, united in a Popular Front solely because of their distaste for his actions. They disliked the president's admiration of the Fascist Axis, the freedom to propagandize he had given the German embassy in Santiago, the brutality with which he had suppressed a strike of railroad workers in 1936. When Alessandri chose Ross as his successor the Popular Front solidified against him.

Still, Ross should have been an easy winner over the Popular Front candidate, Pedro Aguirre Cerda, a lawyer and vintner. But that was the year the ex-dictator Carlos Ibáñez attempted a comeback with the help of the Chilean

Nazis; the young fascists seized a downtown building and fought against government forces. They surrendered to Alessandri's troops—who promptly shot sixty-two of them for no apparent reason. The incident horrified most Chileans. Right-wing supporters of Ross bought votes wholesale, but Aguirre Cerda won by 4000 votes.

The help of the young men led by Frei could have elected Ross. They had backed him but without enthusiasm. When he was defeated the older members of the party denounced Frei. So did conservative priests. The party ordered a reorganization of the *Falange Conservador*, which Frei and the other young men called themselves. But the young men did not wait for that; in November 1938, they resigned from the Conservative party and formed the *Falange Nacional*.

Frei and his group had also been at odds with the Church hierarchy over the Spanish Civil War. For a time the group had sympathized with the corporate-state ideas of the Spanish Falange, but when Franco assumed power sympathy turned to disgust. They could not abide Franco's attempt to blend religion and politics, nor the attack against Jacques Maritain, the French Christian Democrat, by Franco's people, nor the Church's assertion that Franco's was a "holy war." The young Chileans' susbsequent support of the republicans provoked Church disapproval that persisted after the war and finally became official in 1947, when José María Caro, Archbishop of Santiago, issued a blistering attack against them: "This group of *Falange Nacional* that pretends to be formed by Catholics does not merit the confidence of the Church. It is fighting the Franco regime, the most Catholic in the world; in this fight it is allied with the Communists; it also believes in diplomatic and commercial relations with Russia."

By that point, conservative clergymen were also outraged

by the Falange's progressive social program. One bishop, a Monsignor Salinas, publicly accused the group of being "sellers of Christ" to achieve political ends. He did not mention Frei by name, but there was no doubt whom he had principally in mind.

The Sunday following the attack on him, Frei appeared in the cubicle of a priest, a close friend, before mass. He had often come to talk to the priest at this hour; always before he had been with his children.

"Where are the kids?" the priest asked.

"They're at home," Frei said. "I'm afraid to take them out with me."

"Afraid?" the priest asked, surprised.

"I'm afraid that someone hired by the Church will call me a 'seller of Christ,'" Frei said. Then he burst into tears.

As the priest tried to console him, Frei exclaimed, "Always people have said that I was a good man. Now I understand why. I never hated. But now I hate. They have put poison in my soul. Who are *they*? The ecclesiastical authorities."

The attack continued. A priest issued a declaration saying that Frei was an enemy of the Church, and took steps to have him excommunicated. Other clergymen opposed the priest, and the fight was carried all the way to Giovanni Battista Montini, then a Vatican official, now Pope Paul VI.

For Frei the argument was as painful and basic as that of a young man with a father he loves, but with whose ideas he disagrees. He felt that the old Conservative party no longer represented either the best of Catholic thought or offered a valid answer for the needs of Chile. He knew too that the strong anticlerical tradition among Masons focused in the Radical party would naturally create suspicion of any political movement related to Catholicism or its principles. He could see the growth of the Marxist groups day-by-day in Chile. Yet he believed that Catholicism contained a mighty social doctrine. Frei had been attracted to intellectual Catholic movements in Europe, notably that of Jacques Maritain in France. "Religious expression is personal," he once told me. "Each man chooses his own elaboration." By this he meant that while the true conservative could find his view elaborated in Catholicism, he, Frei, might find a viewpoint as liberal as that of Leo XIII.

In one meeting we had he kept stressing the significance of Christianity in stopping the spread of communism. He insisted that only the Christian mentality of Europe had kept it from going communist after World War II. He believed that Chile's only chance lay in this same direction.

But it had to be the "new" Catholic viewpoint; the old, he thought, was useless. At a 1962 conference in Bahia, Brazil, Frei formalized the comparison that evolved in the 1930's:

> There is one version of the theoretical ethos of Catholic theology which we consider to be a deviation but which, at one time, was passed on to the Latin American Catholic by what we might call the Spanish stream of spirituality, which is inconsistent with some of the features of the development ethos. This version is characterized by the following:
>
> 1. The presentation of existing social and economic structures as the will of God, as authorized by divine authority, and therefore the condemnation of any more or less radical change.
>
> 2. Disinterest in material goods, an almost exclusive concentration on the life to come, and indifference to present life.
>
> 3. Resignation to one's own and other people's misery or want, and emphasis on the necessary imperfection of social organisms as a consequence of original sin.
>
> 4. Fatalism as regards man's ability to control and transform his environment—leaving everything "in God's hands."
>
> 5. Emphasis on the goodness of intention, and disregard

of practical effectiveness and the functional value of good intentions.

6. Charity, taken to mean "favoring" certain peoples because of their needs or personal links with them.

7. Emphasis on the cultural, spiritual and Christian humanistic values, and contempt for more material occupations.

However, another version of the theoretical ethos of Catholic theology underlies the lay Christian institutions to which we referred above. This derives mainly from the Franco-Belgian Christian theology and philosophy, which seems to us to be clearly favorable to the development ethos and which has obviously been strengthened by the teaching of the popes and by the encyclical *Mater et Magistra*. This version of the Catholic ethos is characterized by the following:

1. A favorable attitude toward change, since Christian morality is a morality of specific replies to specific problems, which are always different, and thus requires a dynamism that continuously adapts the Christian reply to the problems of existence.

2. A concern with present life, in which the future life has a stake, and a concern which also extends to the material and the physical.

3. Resignation only to the inevitable, but a bitter struggle to adapt existence and its structures in order to improve them, i.e., to make them consistent with a life of union, harmony and love.

4. The conviction that to leave things "in God's hands" does not imply renouncing personal responsibility or a slackening in the effort to achieve change, but only a cautious uncertainty concerning the success of endeavor and its real effectiveness in view of the congenital limitation of knowledge and technique, which are always susceptible of improvement.

5. The inadequacy of good intention by itself. It is particularly important for the Christian to be effective in his action, because his object is not to make use of his neighbor in order to show an ineffective good disposition but to love him in endeavoring to satisfy his needs.

6. Charity directed towards people and potentially towards

all mankind and the common good; this excludes all nepotism or personal considerations in the allocation of productive resources. One loves one's neighbor more by assigning the posts, in enterprises producing goods or services, to the most competent people than by assigning them to those who need them most or are most thankful for them.

7. Deeply respectful consideration for all the range of human activities, including the economic activities of manual worker, employee, businessman and moneylender. All are contributors to the common good, or can become so, and the handling of money does not in itself degrade anyone. It is possible to establish a genuine "spirituality of economic development," or a Christian mystique of the various functions of the productive process. . . .

"To encourage social, political, and in general, human development is, in the long run, to encourage economic development; to obstruct social and political development is to obstruct economic development," Frei noted. The Church, he said "supported the predominant social structures; it defended the political regime in power during the colonial era, with all the abuses of the metropolitan power and restrictions on international trade. . . ." In addition, said Frei, the Church exhibited a "tendency to preserve the status quo, very common among the economically powerful Catholic groups; bewilderment as regards economic and social problems, together with a marked conservative bias at certan levels of the Church hierarchy and the Latin American clergy, or the clergy working in Latin America."

Anguishing it might have been, but Frei's critical stance against conservative elements of the Church was crucial to his political future. To Chileans suspicious of the political motives of the Catholic hierarchy, he had to prove that a political party could be Christian without being confessional. At the same time, he had to demonstrate that Christian Democracy applied to Latin American problems. Thus began his attempt to Chileanize the social Christian philosophy expressed by Jacques Maritain.

Such ideas seem tame today, but in the Chile of the 1930's and 1940's they were a radical departure from existing styles. They appealed mightily to frustrated Conservatives and disillusioned Marxists, and brought many of them to Frei's side.

Frei spoke of humanizing the economic function of man. Instead of being a cipher in an impersonal, dehumanizing process, a worker would be involved in the management of his industry through workers' councils, and by helping to elect company directors. Industry would not pass to the state, but each worker would through an enforced profit-sharing plan participate as an owner of the industry that employed him. Frei described the potential effects of such a plan in a book he published in 1958:

> If we could imagine a vast process of universal extension of property through the organized acquisition of shares by the worker, not in the limited context of the old worker-stockholder, but a planned and large-scale access of labor to capital, we could imagine a social organization in which man would participate in the economic process in two ways—as worker, by his salary, and as owner of capital, through profit. This process ought not to be thought of solely as limited to the enterprise in which the worker is employed, but applied to any enterprise, since the important thing would be to give the worker property, and more than that, to involve him in the process of capitalization, which is the foundation of the economic process, the condition of stability for the worker himself, and the sole form that offers the possibility of raising his standard of living.
>
> This would require action that would make it easy for organized savings to go into investment, something that could not occur without a more equitable distribution. . . .

The state would act to limit the size of economic power, but the state itself would not be permitted to become impersonal. Every effort would be made to involve men in the political as well as the economic process. Intermediate groups would be set up between the individual and the state to facilitate regular contact. Municipally-owned industry would be promoted, administration of government decentralized, stronger municipal government encouraged.

Frei's sense of man's dynamic nature stirred Chile's professional class. Man, he said, need not suffer hell on earth in preparation for eternal life. Not only can man affect his environment; social Christian doctrine compels him to try. K. H. Silvert would later report that Frei's "great appeal to the engineers, architects, economists, and other professionals lies precisely here: he has pointed to a wide and easily recognizable group of pressing difficulties, and he has said that Chilean technicians applying Chilean-oriented techniques toward Chilean appreciations of good and bad will work for national solutions. For these persons his appeal to a romantic and impersonal nationalism within a democratic framework has served to override the clericalism hinted at within the Christian Democratic rubric."

Still another factor worked in Frei's behalf. The post-World War II concern over communism, fostered by the emerging evidence of aggressive Russian designs, had frightened certain Chileans. In 1948 the Gonzalez Videla government, beset by internal difficulties with the Chilean Communists, seized on a dubious incident to break relations with all Communist countries. For "proof" of external meddling, it offered a letter from the Yugoslavian chargé d'affaires to his wife, in which the diplomat commented on strikes in coal mines and referred to Chilean workers as "these Indians." Using this as an excuse, a government with conservative views outlawed the Communist party with the "Law for the Permanent Defense of Democracy." Under its provisions, persons convicted of being Communists or of carrying on "Communist activities" could be sent to detention camps. If the action against the Communist party had bothered many democratic-minded Chileans, the proposed action against individuals offended them. Frei fought the proposal relentlessly. His stand won him the support of many liberals.

In such ways did the third position sow its fields. But the first harvests were thin. Twice Frei lost elections for deputy, the first time in 1937 in Tarapacá, the second time in 1941 in Santiago. Other Falange candidates did no better.

Frei had married in 1935 and in the following years he supported his family with legal fees. His principal client was a nitrate company. As his reputation grew, he received a number of commercial offers. One, a lucrative position in a bank, made him pause. His family was growing—he would have seven children in all—and he needed money. There was not yet any solid evidence that he could succeed in politics. "If I take the offer," he thought, "I'll have to spend the rest of my life chasing *plata*." He decided to stick to principle, and turned the offer down.

In 1945 Frei was named minister of public works in the federal government. Finally in 1949 he won public office; he was elected on the Falange Nacional ticket to the Senate from Atacama and Coquimbo. But he had scant company in Congress.

At midpoint in the 1950's the party began to gain strength. "There is a certain sort of magic in the growth of ideas," Radomiro Tomić remembers poetically. "As it happens with trees in springtime, suddenly they are covered, they are green." In 1948 a small group of progressive members of the Conservative party had broken away from the traditionalists; in 1953 this group allied itself with the *Falange Nacional*. But the magic moment for Frei, the party, and as it later developed, for Chile, came in 1956; President Carlos Ibáñez, who had made an astonishing political comeback in the election of 1952, asked Frei to form a government. Frei, a vigorous critic of the president, was incredulous. He pressed Ibáñez for some clue. The president seemed genuine. He wanted Frei to furnish not simply a cabinet, but a program.

The news stunned political Chile. Frei consulted with his closest friends, to most of whom the offer resembled a Trojan Horse. Ultimately, despite their counsel, Frei determined to accept. "If I don't," he told his worried friends, "I will have forfeited my right to criticize the government. Whenever I open my mouth against them in the Senate, they'll say, 'We gave him the chance, and he turned it down. He has no right to talk.' "

In the meantime, however, horrified conservatives had descended on Ibáñez. Just as Frei was preparing his answer Ibáñez summoned him and told him that "circumstances had changed." He was withdrawing his offer.

But the publicity had irrevocably altered Chile's political balance. Frei was no longer simply another senator from the North. Overnight he had become a national figure. In the election of 1957 he was overwhelmingly reelected to the Senate, this time from Santiago, and with more votes than any other candidate.

The 1957 election ended whatever speculation there had been within the Christian Democratic party about who was to be its presidential candidate. From all sections of the party, members came forward to tell Frei that he must run for the presidency in 1958 to put the party on the political map.

That same year the Falange dissolved the federation with the former Conservative party members and proclaimed itself the Christian Democratic party.

The campaign went poorly. He spoke in terms that were too difficult for all but university groups to understand. And he spoke too close to the truth. "We must go through very difficult times," he would say. "I can't promise you anything. If you don't agree with this, then don't vote for me." At one point in the campaign his manager, Edmundo Pérez, told him his cause was hopeless. Frei had done poorly in the most recent poll, the party had lost a by-election, and they were broke. Pérez advised Frei to withdraw. "I'm going to continue," Frei said. A few weeks later, he traveled to Concepción, a big city to the south. This time, inspired by a tremendous crowd, he reached the people. In Santiago the financiers hedged their bets; with the new contributions, Frei could finish the race.

He came in third, with 20.7 percent of the vote, but he had won what he most wanted—a base for 1964. "Next time," he announced to his friends, "it will be our turn."

The Making of Frei

As the Communist and Western worlds blustered and killed to determine the political fate of man Chile, in free and scrupulous process, considered the prospect of a Marxist society. Never, anywhere, had it happened this way. But here, in Chili, it could. A Socialist, Dr. Salvador Allende, candidate of the *Frente Revolucionario de Acción Popular*, a left-wing coalition of Communist, Socialist, National Democratic and Vanguardia parties known as FRAP, had lost in 1958 by a mere 33,500 votes. The winner, Jorge Alessandri Rodríguez, son of the former president and candidate of the middle and upper classes, was prohibited by the Chilean constitution from seeking reelection. Allende had polled more male votes than any other candidate; only the women had defeated him. Since 1958 he had worked ceaselessly to broaden the base of his support. In the 1961 congressional election, the FRAP coalition had revealed impressive new strength in rural areas. As the election of 1964 approached, political analysts agreed that this time Allende could win.

His victory would mean the basic reordering of Chilean society. All large landholdings would be expropriated by the state; a new system of state and private farms would be established. All minerals would become state property; mining facilities would be nationalized. So would utilities, banking and insurance companies. The rich would be heavily taxed; proceeds would be invested by the state, thereby automatically achieving a redistribution of income. The government would control the distribution of consumer goods. Chile would free herself of military commitments to the U.S. and adopt an attitude of wary pugnacity toward the colossus. Chile would actively support Cuba in hemispheric and world councils.

The international implications were even more sizable. Victory would mean, first, the vindication of Nikita Khrushchev's theory of peaceful revolution; second, the intrusion of Marxism into the hemisphere, not on an isolated island, but in a respected mainland country; third, an end to U.S. influence in Chile, and a loss of influence throughout the hemisphere; fourth, the loss of a billion-dollar U.S. assistance investment; fifth, the expropriation of U.S. firms worth hundreds of millions; and sixth, the kinds of international political explosions that any or all of these elements could produce.

Under normal circumstances, Marxist absolutes were anathema to the individualistic, spiritual Chileans. But by 1964 "normal" had become insufferable. Time and again Chileans had elected the candidates of the traditional parties, and time and again the machinery of government had floundered. Even President Alessandri, the Chilean father figure, could not make the machine work for the people. The rich were getting richer, the poor poorer. To the average Chilean, government seemed like a private club, its benefits for members only. The government granted capitalists liberal credit for speculative investment; the government collected little revenue from tax-evading Chilean producers. Huge deficits resulted. The escudo depreciated. Inflation ground the poor man down.

Agricultural production was not increasing as fast as the birthrate; by 1963 the cost of food was seven times what it had been in 1955 and was still rising faster than wages. For lack of funds, school construction was off; Chile, which prides itself on having one of the highest literacy rates in Latin America, could find no classrooms for 300,000 children. "We have voted for people who were rich," a bearded ragpicker told a U.S. reporter, "and they have done nothing. Now it is time to vote for people who are poor."

For the Communists, the election of 1964 was to be the payoff for more than forty years of careful work. They had preached the legal road to power. In Chile the Socialists have traditionally been of a more revolutionary mind than the Communists; had it not been for the Communists, the Socialists might have attempted violent overthrow of the government years before. But patience had been the Communists' counsel, and over the years it had seemed to work. Except for the ten years between 1948 and 1958, when the party was outlawed, it had flourished in a democratic climate. Communists served in Congress; Communists had once served in the federal cabinet.

For tactical reasons the Communists had chosen to remain in the background, but they had considerable strength. They numbered 32,000 loyal and well-trained members and had access to places of power. Their basic strength was in union organizations. As the election of 1964 approached, the Communists controlled major segments of the Central Union of Chilean Workers (the illegal but real national labor apparatus), the coal, copper, nitrate and construction workers, newspaper kiosk venders, workers in some branches of the chemical drug industry, about one-third of the textile workers and the metal fabricators. Leaderships in steelworkers' unions had shifted from year to year between the Communists and Socialists. The character of the Chilean union movement was highly political; a worker would vote for a candidate for union office because he was a member of the same party, and not necessarily because he might be a good shop steward. Thus union control was a good barometer of political sentiment.

Thousands of teachers at all levels were and are Marxists —some intellectuals, some activists. The selection of materials and the tenor of discussions are both heavily influenced by their presence. The Communist newspaper, *El Siglo*, is excellent by Latin American standards—topical, professional, effective. Communists populate Chile's artistic community; Pablo Neruda, an outstanding Latin American poet, has for years traveled to the mines to read his poetry to workers. In the slums, some 2000 paid organizers mold the poor into political units; Communist "mayors" run several large *callampas*; many of the streets are named after national and international Marxist heroes.

Alone, the Communist party could never hope to win Chile. At its peak in the 1965 parliamentary election, the party's voting strength was 12.9 percent of the total vote. But by its alignment with the Socialists and other radical left-wing groups, the party could more than double its strength. Since candidates have traditionally divided the presidential vote three or more ways, a group with a nucleus of 30 percent of the voters and an appealing candidate could gain power. In Salvador Allende, the Communists—and FRAP—had that candidate.

Allende is just the blend that the lower-class Chilean likes—a radical with status. He is a medical doctor, a member of an excellent upper middle-class family, a man of taste who lives in a good house in a fine suburb, a habitué, until a few years ago, of the aristocratic Club de la Unión, the son of a devout Catholic. But a rebellious strain has marked his life. In the midst of his studies at the University of Chile he had been expelled for political reasons. At an early age he joined the Socialist party. When Chile experimented with a Popular Front government under Pedro Aguirre Cerda, Allende became minister of public health. He has been a Socialist senator since 1945. In 1956 he was instrumental in forming the coalition with the Communists and several small splinter Marxist groups, although the party was officially illegal at the time. Here, then, was a well-to-do Marxist, an accepted member of the professional class who, despite his political view, enjoyed the esteem of the conservative aristocracy.

On paper it never seemed possible that an out-and-out Marxist could win election in Chile. Yet Allende combined personality and circumstance into a potentially successful blend. For all his revolutionary bent, he seemed to have a malleable streak. His critics within the revolutionary ranks would often say that he was not a genuine revolutionary; they pointed out that Allende was never implicated in any of the Socialist military plots. Secondly, he was capable of making subtle changes in his declarations wherever necessary. James Rowe tells how Allende was quoted by a North American newspaper reporter as having said that he did not plan to expropriate American-owned copper companies, but would only nationalize the marketing of copper. "Shortly afterward," Rowe reports, "he received a midnight phone call from Havana, wanting to know 'what's this about?'" After this episode, Allende required certain

American journalists to base their stories on notarized summaries of interviews with him.

Allende insisted that he could Chileanize Marxism. Marxism, he would say, was only a method, not a system, and its applications could have shadings and distinctions according to local conditions. To support his thesis, Allende could point to the many ideological refinements within the once-monolithic Communist world.

Allende was angered by the suggestion that he would be controlled by the Communists. He insisted that FRAP was a "coalition of equals," and that if he were elected president he would not be maneuvered by the Communists. He also maintained that good relations with the United States were not impossible. Everything, he said, depended on the United States. If it respected Chilean sovereignty, Chile might well retain pleasant political, economic and cultural relations with the United States. Where Chile might benefit from American assistance, and where this assistance was offered in friendship and not with compromising conditions, Chile would be happy to accept.

But Allende was committed to the nationalization by expropriation of the American-owned copper mines—and such action would preclude U.S. assistance. As James Rowe points out: "The resulting domestic and international quarrels most likely would push the Allende government in just one direction—and it is naïve to believe the Communists have not learned anything since 1938, when Chile had a Popular Front government."

A major imponderable of the election, however, was the extraordinary change in the electorate. Almost three times as many persons—2.5 million—would vote in 1964 as had voted just twelve years before. Easier registration procedures had attracted many new voters. In addition, the country had been highly politicized in the last several years, particularly in the rural areas. Traditionally these areas had been controlled by *patrónes* of the big estates who, subtly or overtly, influenced the votes of their workers—if and when the workers voted. But since 1952 politicians of all parties had vigorously canvassed the rural areas, and there were many indications that the influence of the *patrón* was disappearing.

Another imponderable was the unpredictable streak in the voter himself. The average Chilean eludes labels; only a minority profess a party affiliation. In 1964 Eduardo Hamuy, director of the Center of Socio-Economic Studies of the University of Chile, questioned Chileans about their political loyalties. More than 90 percent responded that they did not belong to a party.

But if such imponderables might be working for Allende, they might also be working for Frei.

Perhaps never in the history of Latin America had a man and his party prepared so thoroughly for an election. Since 1958 Frei had won many of Chile's best minds to his cause. These men—professionals, industrialists, technicians, teachers—he had gathered into an enormous study and advisory group, divided into areas of specialization. Two years before the election their findings and recommendations had been boiled down by Frei and a group of advisors led by his devoted aide Alavaro Marfán into a comprehensive blue book for the future of Chile.

The book touched every aspect of Chilean life. Its pages were permeated with the Christian Democratic concept of humanizing the situation of man—an abhorrence of the anonymity of both capitalistic materialism and monolithic communism; a belief that man should participate in the state, not as a nameless body, but as a unique being. (This all but theological imperative for man's self-fulfillment is very close to the thinking of the late Protestant theologian Paul Tillich, and the late Jewish theologian Martin Buber.)

Specifically, the program called for government participation in those areas where laissez-faire capitalism had failed to demonstrate initiative or vigor. In agriculture the government would expropriate lands not being used productively, paying the owner 10 percent down and the balance in long-term, 5 percent bonds. The disinterested landowner would be penalized under a taxation system based not on what the farm produced, but on what it *might have* produced. The formation of cooperatives would be stimulated, soil conserved and peasants organized.

Copper, Chile's major dollar-earner, was another target. The Christian Democrats pledged to double production. United States copper companies would continue to function, but the state would take over marketing and sell to all comers.

Taxation would be drastically revised. The collection system would be modernized, and new schedules would make significant demands on the wealthy classes, whose taxes at present were slight.

Great fervor was reserved for the economic integration of Latin America. Without a common market, Latin America, the Christian Democrats declared, could never achieve major power status. The subject of a Latin American common market would preoccupy Frei long after his election. "The integration of Latin America must be the great political objective of our hemisphere," he would declare later, "and . . . the test that will demonstrate the capacity or incapacity of our governments and peoples to define their destiny in this century." He told me once: "We are prepared for such an event, but it's no good for one to do it, and the others not. Others might think that I seek in this a personal glory, or something glorious for Chile, when in reality we feel this very deeply as something that all Latin America needs."

Perhaps the most extensive recommendations were for the overhaul of government itself. Legislative and judicial areas would be modernized and democratized. The presidency would receive more power; a president stymied by Congress could call for a plebiscite to gain approval of his measure. Conflict of interest, always a major problem in a country where almost every professional had at least a part-time job with the government, would be combatted, hopefully eliminated.

The Christian Democratic call was for vigorous reform, and it embodied an appeal to the dormant patriotism and latent social consciousness of the Chileans. The instrument of this appeal was Frei himself. Thirteen months before the election, his campaign already had a pep-rally fervor. Students paraded through the streets, waving signs and singing. Workers rallied in his behalf.

Campaigning in the slums, he was a study in moods. His laugh would boom, but his eyes would brood and his voice sharpen with anger. "How many children?" he asked one young mother.

"Four," she responded.

"Ah, how good. I have seven."

"We need water."

"We are going to help you." Then he turned to the gathering crowd. His smile disappeared. He spoke in an urgent tone: "You have heard enough of promises. I am not going to speak to you of promises. . . ."

He would speak, instead, of change. "There are two

Lefts—the Marxist Left and the Democratic Left," he would say. "We are the Democratic Left. Chile doesn't want a government of the Right. It wants reform. But it doesn't want reform under dictatorship. Ours is a third position—not a transaction between both, but a valid new position."

To professional men he would speak on another level: "We can't survive if we don't have development. We can't have development if we don't change the social structure." He would urge his audience to admit that the benefits of society had eluded the great majority of Chileans. Then he would continue: "We can't change the economic capacity of this country without doing something about the social condition of man."

The first indication that Frei's words were being listened to came in April 1963. Two million Chileans were voting for municipal officials, but the whole country was looking for a trend applicable to the coming presidential election. The results were decisive. The Christian Democrats polled 22.7 percent of the vote, making them the country's single biggest political group. A post-election analysis indicated that the added strength had come primarily from 600,000 new voters, as well as from conservatives dismayed by the continuing erosion of economic conditions, and non-Communist liberals who had had enough of the far Left. Frei was jubilant. "There are three things working in our favor," he told reporters. "First, people are tired of the present political juxtaposition. Second, people don't want a rightist government. Third, people don't want a Communist government."

Frei was still not convinced that he would win the presidency, but as the campaign progressed, he began to feel that he was riding a swelling tide. When this tide would

106

crest he did not know, but that it would one day, he was certain. Once as we were traveling he said suddenly, "Thirty years ago, Christian Democracy was nothing. Ten years ago, Christian Democracy was nothing. But now it is the grand force in Latin America." He paused, regarded me with a twinkle, and added, laughing, "*Caramba*, what a force in Latin America."

Early in 1964 Frei received additional good news. Professor Hamuy had asked a representative sample of Chilean voters which party came the closest to expressing their own ideas. Forty percent had named the Christian Democrats, far more than had named any other party. Hamuy had also asked voters to name the party for which they held a "favorable opinion." Communists and Socialists together had polled 21.9 percent. The Christian Democrats had polled 30.8 percent.

But on that same quesionnaire was a statistic to give Frei pause. A total of 40 percent of the voters had said they favored positions expressed by the Radicals, Liberals or Conservatives—and these three parties were running their own candidate for president, wealthy, forty-five-year-old Radical and political veteran, Julio Durán.

Together the three parties formed a powerful coalition of the "haves." The Conservative party, comprised largely of the landholding aristocracy, had traditionally been favored by the Catholic Church and the conservative clergy. The party had expressed the Catholic position in society, approving church control of the schools and of marriage, and disapproving divorce. The Liberals favored separation of church and state, but otherwise their views were those of the Conservatives. Rich immigrants found their way into the Liberal camp. The Radicals, once militantly anti-Catholic and reform-minded, had lost their fervor in recent years—a tribute to the aristocracy's policy of absorbing any group which threatened them. In 1964 Radicalism was a solid, safe, substantial position, its program more a continuation of past policies than a call to adventure.

As the campaign took shape there were three major forces, any two of which might unite for an easy victory. Rumors abounded. From all sides Frei was pressured to deal with one of the other groups. His refusal was unequivocal: "We can't win with the millionaires. We can't win with the Communists. We alone will win the election."

The turning point in the campaign was an otherwise insignificant by-election for Congress in the rural province of Curicó, in the rich central valley. A Socialist deputy, Oscar Naranjo, had died in office. A new election was scheduled for March 15, 1964. In the 1963 elections the Democratic Front, as the Radical-Liberal-Conservative coalition called itself, had polled almost as many votes as the Christian Democrats and the Marxist FRAP candidates combined. In Curicó they saw an opportunity to demonstrate their strength in a fashion that would have tremendous psychological impact. The decision, for them, was a disaster. The candidate of the Democratic Front, a Conservative, was swamped by the FRAP candidate, Oscar Naranjo's son. The candidate of the Christian Democrats came in third, but the victory was really theirs. Since the Front had predicted a significant victory, defeat was so humiliating that Durán withdrew from the race for president. The coalition then fell apart. (Durán later reentered the race as the Radical candidate, hoping to secure enough votes to prevent a majority and thereby throw the election to Congress where he could bargain away his support in exchange for political advantages in the next government. The Radicals held fifty seats in Congress, enough to throw the election to Allende or Frei.)

It was a difficult time for Liberals and Conservatives. They could now choose either the Marxist or the democratic reformists. There was no doubt about which of the two they saw as the lesser evil. But many of these men loathed Frei, not simply because he had criticized them so severely, but because, having married into a good family, he did not then behave as "good" Chilean men are supposed to, and traditionally do—they work hard, prosper, live well and defend the status quo. President Jorge Alessandri Rodríguez, in particular, disliked Frei because the Senator had severely criticized his policies. Alessandri supporters complained that Frei himself had frustrated the progressive measures the administration had attempted to put through Congress.

But after a short struggle both right-wing parties went over to Frei. They had no other place to go.

Two events followed quickly. A fourth presidential candidate suddenly dropped out of the race. He was Jorge Prat, a former minister of finance now in his mid-forties, a close friend of retiring President Alessandri's, and his personal choice. Prat's campaign had been the most nationalistic of the four; while not a serious threat, it too, like Durán's later candidacy, possessed enough latent strength to be pivotal should the election go to Congress. But with the Liberal and Conservative endorsement of Frei, Prat withdrew.

The second, and ultimately the conclusive development, was the hardening of the Christian Democratic campaign along anti-Communist lines. Historically, Christian Democrats have prided themselves on their tolerance of all viewpoints; they have consistently supported the free functioning of all political groups in Chile (Frei's stand along these lines in the 1930's had won him much favor from liberals and radicals throughout the country.) Now, possibly to clarify the election, possibly because it seemed opportune, possibly simply because it was indeed the reality, the Christian Democrats began to hammer at the idea that the people had a simple choice to make in the election of 1964: the free way, or the Marxist way.

By comparison with their momentary allies from the Right, their appeal was restrained. The Christian Democrats could not control the Conservatives and Liberals—a situation that for them was ideal. They could profit from the attacks on Allende by the Conservatives and Liberals, but they need not take responsibility for them. A well-financed, well-organized, anti-Communist campaign, which increased in tempo almost every day, ultimately overwhelmed Allende. There were allegations, never proven but probably true, that money came from West German Christian Democrats, the West German government, CARITAS (the Catholic relief organization), and of course, the CIA. Intellectuals—Christian Democrats among them—found the campaign offensive, boring and unnecessary, but less sophisticated groups were impressed. Scenes of executions in Cuba were plastered on walls throughout the country. One showed a former Cuban president being shot by soldiers of Castro's army. A favorite poster featured a Russian soldier and Santa Claus. The caption read: "Who do you want to knock at your door this Christmas?"

Letters from well-known Latin American liberals told of the hard life in Cuba. Talks by Cubans who had fled their country were broadcast. In August, a month before the election, right-wing newspapers intensified their efforts to associate Allende's candidacy with the Cuban Communists. The FRAP coalition had insistently denied that it intended to set up a Cuban-style Socialist state. Allende swore that there were differences between Chile and Cuba, and insisted that his government would only be a transitional step leading eventually to socialism. But the newspapers managed to dig up earlier, incriminating statements. One newspaper quoted a Socialist, Oscar Nuñez, as favoring mass executions, if necessary, to carry out reforms.

How far the attack had gone was revealed by an incident that took place three weeks before the election. On August 11, Chile broke diplomatic relations with Cuba in accordance with sanctions voted by the OAS. Frei termed the action "profoundly inopportune," and promised to review it. But Allende said nothing; his objection would have appeared to confirm press reports that as president he would apply Cuban-style measures to Chile.

On August 15 a personal and tragic element was added to the campaign. Frei's dynamic sister, his right arm, as he called her, was killed instantly in an automobile collision at a Santiago intersection. Her body was taken to the Hospital El Salvador in Santiago. There, Frei, surrounded by his family, wept inconsolably the entire morning.

The effect on Chile was overwhelming. For several days the campaign halted. It was as though the entire country had been drawn into the Frei family circle. On the day of the funeral a mass of Chileans lined the streets to view the funeral procession. Frei, his eyes clouded, his brow knit, his face unable to mask his pain, led his family. As the cortege passed, the silent thousands threw flowers in tribute.

Several days later the campaign resumed. Frei went to Ñuñoa, a big district within Santiago. Thirty thousand persons heard him begin: "I cannot speak with joy. All that is gone. I can only promise...."

111

After several days the hiatus in venom ended, and the attacks on Allende began anew. Newspapers published a letter to Allende from a Cuban, Manuel Urrutia, who had been Cuba's first president in the Castro regime. His experience, he wrote, qualified him to know the dangers of cooperating with the Communists. He begged Allende to "choose Chile over Russia." The night before the election, conservative-owned radio stations broadcast an appeal from Fidel Castro's sister, who had defected and now bitterly opposed her brother. Since campaigning was supposed to end the previous midnight, the government permitted Allende to respond immediately by radio to the attack.

Election day, September 4, began warily. There had been talk of violence. Soldiers were out in force. United States citizens had been instructed to remain in their homes. But the Chilean sense of fair play prevailed and there were no incidents. By 4 P.M., when the polls closed, the soldiers were leaning on their rifles in boredom.

The trend for Frei developed with the first returns. At 8 P.M. the Christian Democrats lowered a blackboard out a window in party headquarters in downtown Santiago, and the crowd in the street roared. Frei was leading by 400,000 votes.

As the figures piled up for Frei, his supporters paraded jubilantly down the streets, waving torches, banging rhythmically on their cars, "*Viva, viva, viva* Frei." The shouts traveled all the way to Allende headquarters, where a dejected crowd of a thousand waited in the street. There, at 8:35 P.M., Allende, his face set, emerged from a conference with his chiefs to address the crowd. As his aides wept, Allende, speaking with difficulty, urged his supporters to accept his defeat calmly and with dignity.

The final tally was Frei: 1,418,101; Allende: 982,122;

Durán: 125,122. Among men, Frei and Allende had polled almost evenly. Among women, Frei polled 744,423 votes; Allende only 375,766. Women thus favored Frei by 368,657 votes, giving him not simply the election, but a majority and a mandate. With their help he had demolished the Marxist coalition and all but destroyed the country's conservative parties.

Late that evening Frei spoke to his delirious supporters from party headquarters. His speech was brief and emotional. He paid tribute to his dead sister and embraced his family. Then he adjourned to his house where the mood soon became hilarious. The Chilean dinner-hour is dramatically late, about 10 P.M., but this night it was even later in the Frei household; so many close friends attended that dinner guests sat two to a chair. Suddenly, Frei startled the group. "Maruja!" he called sternly to his wife, who was sitting at the other end of the table. "Stand up!" His face was solemn, forbidding. Puzzled, Mrs. Frei stood. Then Frei commanded, "Sit down." Frowning, she sat. Frei pounded his fist on the table. "Now," he shouted, "*I* am the boss." In the uproar that followed, the loudest laugh was the president-elect's.

6

President Frei

A transfer of political power renews a nation. The past is dead. Possibility is king. The people reclaim destiny. Such was the mood of Chile as Eduardo Frei took office on November 3, 1964.

For weeks the sense of renewal had been building. From North and South, from the high mountains and the long shore, the Chilean people had converged on the capital. There, as the inaugural drew near, music blared, costumed peasants danced in the streets and wine flowed at neighborhood block-parties. Each night the city blazed with fireworks and spotlights played on government buildings. Each day scores of diplomats, many in exotic dress, arrived to pay homage to the new leader, sirens screamed and limousines raced through the streets. Flags of all nations billowed in the fresh spring breeze. As they felt the gaze of the world upon them, the Chileans walked with heads a little higher, chests a little fuller. "What do you think of our country *now*?" a stranger asked a passing American. It was a time to remember that all men are brothers, and in his inaugural address President Frei struck this note.

"I salute the friendly people of the United States," he said, "part of our great America, in which we wish a true association in equal dignity that is not born in the unbalance of power and wealth, but in a true alliance that permits our progress in liberty, as indicated by a man who died but whose message continues even more alive and present. . . . I salute also from here the people of the so-called Socialist world, from whose dramatic human adventure we cannot be estranged, which other people do not ignore, and which it would be blind on our part to ignore, even though profound ideological differences may separate us. . . . Without their coexistence peace could not prevail."

To his people, Frei spoke with a cadence and fervor reminiscent of the American President he had so admired:

I am here to give education to all the children of Chile, and to open to them all the opportunities, without another limit than their own capacity, in the certainty that a people that overcomes ignorance inevitably defeats misery and servitude.

I am here in order that, increasingly, the farmers may be owners of the land, and property may not be confined in a few hands; in order that those who work in the fields may have a just income and salary, and that the laws that defend them may be rigorously enforced.

I am here in order that all the families in Chile may live in a modest house, but their own, in a decent neighborhood where their children can grow with dignity and happiness.

I am here in order to promote economic development and to stimulate the creative spirit and free initiative of Chileans so that we may increase food production and take advantage of the resources of the sea and the forests; in order that we may expand our industries and exploit our mineral resources to the benefit of Chile, whose interest must always be the supreme law.

I am here to stop inflation, to defend the value of our

money, to give steady employment and to open opportunity to young Chileans.

I am here to achieve the development of human and family welfare, of technical capacity and economic potential through an authentic popular promotion.

I am here in order to break the rigidity of a social order that does not respond yet to the demands of the time and to open to the people a progressive access to culture, to the responsibility in government and true participation in the richness and in the advantages that characterize the affluent societies.

His expression stern, the president of Chile declared: "If anyone believes that my words were banners to gain power and to keep it afterward, he is mistaken. The banners answer a faith and a conviction, and they will not be abandoned."

To the cynical listener, such words might have been taken for rhetoric. Those who know Frei knew he spoke the truth. "He's the only really moral modern man I've ever known," a wide-ranging diplomat and close friend of Frei's told me once. "He's close to the Maritain ideal. I place him among the first ten leaders of the world. This is a universal man."

Most foreigners meeting Frei are profoundly impressed by his sincerity and drive. One day in February 1964, Frei lunched at the Hotel Crillon in Santiago with Gardner Cowles, the editor in chief of *Look*, who was on a fact-finding trip through Latin America. After lunch Cowles, who has made such trips annually to all parts of the world, observed: "I've met hundreds of politicians in my day. That man's the most impressive politician I've met in years." Senator Eugene J. McCarthy of Minnesota, a staunch admirer, noted: "When he gets to talking about the poor and the need for social justice, you begin to feel

116

that spiritual drive that makes him such a compelling person."

Yet, ironically, the very spiritual drive that enthralls foreigners has always been a grave handicap for Frei at home. He suffers from a charge of saintliness. He is too nice for politics, his critics argue, and Frei's closest friends acknowledge the problem. "He was a bad candidate," one of them confides. "He was very frank. He didn't like the facile promise. He didn't like the smallness of the political game. He was violently attacked by the political sectors, and the attacks had their effect."

The real Frei is not at all saintly. Rather, he is an intensely human man who relishes a good cigar, and a whiskey, and occasionally flames with anger. To the picture of the cool Swiss must be added that of the incendiary Latin rushing from his car to chase some workers who had alluded vulgarly to his nose. Then there is Frei the incorrigible practical joker, who will call friends and in a false voice announce some calamitous news. Arriving for dinner at the home of friends one evening he approached Javier Lagarrigue, and with a face as inscrutable as a basset's said: "Javier, you really must have done something terrible to someone. Your four tires are completely flat." Lagarrigue ran angrily to his car, only to return red-faced moments later and find Frei weak from laughter.

Frei has not allowed his rise to power to cut him off from his friends. I recall one afternoon in his office at *La Moneda* in August 1965, almost a year after he had become president. He was in the midst of his worst crisis to date. His copper bill was in trouble in Congress, and since all of his financial plans hinged on this one act, the president was working determinedly behind the scenes to push it through. Our own conversations would frequently be interrupted by an urgent call from the floor of Congress. One such call reported that some Radical deputies were in an uproar over a certain provision. His face pinched in concentration, Frei thought for a moment, then dealt out strategy for his lieutenants to follow. The moment he finished, Frei took another priority call. "Carmen?" he began. "How are the children?"

Nor has power itself changed his values. To this day he cannot take his palace seriously. One day, as we were walking down a long palace-corridor to tea, I asked him what he had thought when he had first sat behind the presidential desk.

"You mean," he said, "what did I feel?"

"Yes," I said.

"In truth?"

"In truth."

"I had the feeling I'd been here a long, long time." And then, in front of a smiling palace-guard, the president of Chile sent a boom of laughter through the sedate palace-halls.

Frei has steadfastly refused to move his family to the palace, preferring to remain in his modest, middle-class house. His refusal upsets some Chileans, who interpret the action as a loss of dignity and style. "It's just like Chile to have elected a Swiss president," taunts novelist José Donoso. "What's he afraid of?" As we were walking to tea, I asked Frei why he continued to live at home. He shrugged. "What kind of a place is this to raise children?" he asked. "It's too open, too big. The children couldn't live a normal life. I don't want them to live a false life—particularly in this phase of their lives. I want them to grow up simply. Look, when they go to school, they don't go in the presidential car. I don't permit it. They go by public bus. As for

me, when I leave here at 8:30 P.M., I want to be myself."
He waved his arms at the lofty drapes and dark portraits
and heavy chandeliers. "I couldn't be myself here."

Mrs. Frei reinforces her husband's desire for simplic-
ity. Shortly after the inauguration she told a magazine reporter who interviewed her at her home: "We don't want
to lose independence. It will be easier to conserve the in-
timacy of family life here than there." Since Frei's inauguration, the first lady has found it difficult to accustom herself to her new role. One day, a friend, observing her drive
up to the presidential palace, arrived in time to hear her
ask a guard if it was all right to park for five minutes while
she ran inside to speak to her husband.

Neither money nor what money buys has ever really
interested Frei. He did not own an automobile until he was
thirty-five. During the campaign, when he frequently en-
tertained important people in his home, party officials worried that Frei's help was not able to provide the kind of
dinner and service to which the guests were accustomed.
They suggested that Frei hire a special staff and pay them
with party funds. Frei refused. (The president gives Mrs.
Frei, who has never in her life signed a check, a fixed sum
each week to run the household.) Even today, Frei is still
so economically pressed that friends must be careful not to
put him in an awkward position. On returning from trips
they bring him no more than a tie, lest he feel compelled to
reciprocate.

Frei's attitude toward money is expressed best, perhaps,
in an incident which occurred when he was a young father
with several children. A close friend was on the verge of a
business foreclosure. Frei told him: "The only thing I have
is my house, but if you need it for security, it's yours." Says
the friend today: "I first would have died."

119

Frei's modesty is genuine; it has not been overcome by the panoply of the presidency. On his return from his triumphant tour of Europe, he told his people:

When in the great capitols of old Europe there waved the tricolor flags with their star and their blue, their white and their red, when I heard the military bands of these nations playing the anthem of *our* nation, when I saw how the crowds and their governments received the president of this faraway nation, I asked myself, "What is happening? What are they applauding? Are they applauding Mr. Eduardo Frei, who has passed so many times without recognition?" No. They were applauding the 150 years of clean Chilean history; they were applauding our democracy and our liberty, in which the president of the republic can walk among his people without fear of anyone. They were applauding the maturity of this people who, in an election that has stirred the world, . . . gave a lesson, indicated a path, traced a route for Latin America . . . and the members of the governments of all Europe told me openly, "You are tracing . . . a path for democracy and for the world." . . . That is what they applauded.

Such modesty in a politician is rare and becoming. Yet it can be troublesome as well. For a politician must be willing to use all the powers at his disposal, and there is an inherent reserve in this regard with Frei. Once, eleven months after his election, I asked him if he thought he had developed charisma. He pondered the question before answering, and it was evident that the idea troubled him. "Yes, I guess so," he said at last. "What do you think?" I told him that I had found an intense belief in his person among many Chileans. He thought about that, and said: "I'm not the sort of person who wants anything constructed for me. But I recognize that I have a certain personal following. I want to utilize it, not to exalt my person, but to achieve certain ends to help my program."

Frei is loathe to impose on others. In 1963, after a conference at the University of Notre Dame, he met secretly
with President Kennedy. Kennedy, a great admirer of Frei,
expressed sympathy for Frei's objectives, and told him he
was working hard to arouse support among the American
people for an enlightened policy toward Latin America. A
U.S. diplomat who attended the meeting told me later:
"Although Frei represented a political party oriented specifically toward the Catholic religion, he did not attempt to
play upon President Kennedy's Catholicism to establish
rapport with him. This was a restraint not always exercised
by visitors from Latin America."

One day in 1965, Frei attended a ceremony commem-
orating the opening of a governmental reforestation program.
The ceremony, attended by all the foreign diplomats, was
agonizingly long. Afterward, one of the diplomats seethed:
"Can you imagine a minister of agriculture making his president sit in public and listen to thirty-five minutes of his ideas
concerning reforestation?"

The dichotomous quality that Frei brings to politics was
best described to me one day in 1965 by a close friend of
the president's:

> I have two things to say about Eduardo Frei, one un-
> favorable, the second favorable. Unfavorable: He has a great
> respect for people. Favorable: He is indecisive. I know this
> sounds paradoxical, but let me explain. He respects everyone.
> This is very bad. For him to serve well as president, he must
> be able to throw out the people who are not doing their job.
> Those who serve him well, he should keep. Those who fail,
> he should throw out. When Eduardo finds weakness in his
> ministers, he's going to lose a lot of sleep, because he will be
> loathe to throw them out. This is very bad in government.
>
> The favorable quality is his indecision. In the campaign,
> they said he believed what the last person told him. There's

much truth in this. He's completely open. That enables him to hear all sides. On the little things, it's true he can be persuaded. That's good, that's human. But in the basic line, the basic direction, he has a solidity, a thrust, a tranquility. On the basic idea of where he's going, nothing will change him. He's hard, he's firm. He doesn't even wish to discuss it.

Another who knows Frei well amplifies the point. "He's a typical intellectual, a typical analyst—an Adlai Stevenson. Those who say he's *zig-zigiante* are wrong. He's not *zig-zigiante*. He's *balanceado*. He sees the pros and cons, and it's difficult for him to make a decision. He's always shocked when he's made up his mind. But once he's made it up, he's terribly strong. Not only strong. Hard."

As Frei gains more experience in office the doubts about his ability to overcome his tenderness are beginning to vanish. When one recent U.S. visitor suggested warily that certain Christian Democratic candidates for office lacked quality, Frei responded, "Bad? They're miserable!" At one point in the first year of his administration, a certain deputy was giving him a great deal of trouble. Frei assured a concerned diplomat that while the deputy might speak against him, in a showdown he would vote for the Frei program. "There are a lot of familiar relationships to deal with," Frei confided. "There are ways of handling Congress. This man's brother is an ambassador. He will stay an ambassador." Nor has the Frei government been averse to using pressure where it felt the pressure would work. At one point it withdrew government ads from a newspaper that was criticizing the Frei program. The paper got the message.

Foreigners who work closely with Frei believe that on balance he offers exceptional promise. They acknowledge that there are areas of his thinking that would be hard to change. Frei is convinced, for example, of the basic iniquity and selfishness of most bankers and wealthy landowners. He has a built-in bias toward schemes that are imaginative, and is less responsive to those that are practical, a legacy from the Latin side of his heritage. But the Swiss influence is present too. While Frei is frequently emotional about some issues, he is nonetheless systematic; he takes things apart, laboriously trying to see where each piece fits. He can be persuaded and will listen to reason. For example, Frei thought U.S. assistance should be extensive and was disappointed when he learned the actual amount would be lower than he had expected. When the technical reasons for the lower figure were elaborated, however, he quickly perceived—and accepted—the logic.

The overriding impression of Frei is that he is proving to be a strong president. To an extent that could not reasonably be expected, he has resisted pressures from his party for a big social program with great political appeal. For all his tenderness and taste, he can be very cold in handling a situation. I once asked a friend of Frei's to explain how he managed to be as effective as he was. "By the way he can keep silent," the friend responded. "He is a man who listens much. He can stay an hour, an hour and a half, and say two words."

Eduardo Frei would need every resource he could summon to office. For by November 1964, Chile was in a state of stagnation. Between 1960 and 1962 the country's average annual increase in national product had been 5.7 percent; by 1964 the increase had dipped to about 3.1 percent —not nearly enough for a country requiring dramatic growth. In addition, Chile was caught in the persistent tide of an inflation that had not ebbed for a hundred years. The money young Eduardo Frei had used to buy his middle-class Santiago home would be worth $80 today. In the 1960–62 period, living costs had been held to an annual 11 percent increase. But in 1963 the cost of living had risen by 45 percent, and would do so again in 1964. The rate of inflation had thus quadrupled—as had the government's deficits, prime cause of the rise. Government expenses accounted for close to one-third of the Gross National Product. The national debt was $1.7 billion; servicing it cost $300 million annually. To pay its bills, the government had been forced to the printing presses; by 1964 Chilean currency was worth one-third of its value in 1962.

A new tax system was desperately needed. Property taxes were ridiculously small. Income taxes provided but 18 percent of the country's tax revenues.

Food costs were rising 45 percent annually. Chile was spending one-sixth of its scarce dollar income to import food it might easily have raised itself. Of 35 million acres of land suitable for agriculture, only 7.5 million were in use, only 4 million irrigated. Somehow, Frei would have to find a way to dynamize the agricultural society. He would need to acquire those lands not in productive use, through a program of land reform. He would need, as well, a program of credits, technical assistance, co-operatives, mechanization. Both projects would impose a new strain on Chile's already overextended financial resources.

As Frei took office, one-third of the Chilean people had no purchasing power, were all but unemployable and made no contribution to the money economy. About ten percent of employable Chileans were without jobs. Underemployment was severe. And just to maintain this wholly unsatisfactory status, 100,000 new jobs would have to be created each year.

Within government the problem was the opposite—overemployment. The payroll for 400,000 public employees accounted for 24.04 percent of the entire national budget. In the fiscal sector alone, there were 158,300 employees, about one for every fifty Chileans. The bureaucracy was expensive, wasteful and inefficient—it could be run with 30 percent fewer people—but modernizing it was not the simple matter it seemed. A man fired from a government job might not find another in job-scarce Chile. He would then become a costly ward of the state. Moreover, under liberal pre-Frei retirement laws, a sacked civil servant can be as great a drain on the budget as one who continues on the payroll. Government is the biggest employer in Chile; a large-scale trimming of the bureaucracy could have serious economic aftereffects.

In a society where jobs are neither numerous nor adequately paid, government bureaucracy is an infinitely more complex political matter than in the United States. Basically Chileans are a law-abiding people who do not enter government poor and exit rich. Chilean graft, if it can be called that, is to use government as a sinecure. Government employment is a Chilean's dream: once he has it he never loses it. Anyone with any kind of education—be he a doctor, lawyer, professor, or even an artist—seeks some kind of government retainer. The economic consequences are grave. As one bystander put it: "This is a cow everybody milks and nobody feeds." A government employee may retire on full salary after thirty years. Any increases paid after his retirement to persons in his rating are also passed on to him. Because service in foreign posts rates an extra year's credit toward retirement, the effect is to shorten the time of active employment for certain Chileans to twenty or twenty-five years. Some government employees who began as messengers at the age of sixteen are "retired"

125

on full pension by their mid-thirties, working at something else. In Chile today, the number of persons drawing pensions is as great as the number working.

Anyone obtaining a job through the good offices of a political party traditionally kicks back a portion of his salary to the party's war chest. Thus, a party in power has a means of self-perpetuation. In his first months in office, Frei found many Christian Democrats eager to make use of the apparatus.

Politics and finance would also complicate the delicate task of building a partnership between the government of Chile and the American copper companies—a historic proposal put forward by Frei in his first months in office. For years it had been open knowledge that the Americans had maintained cordial relations with the party in power through such devices as the strategic placement of allied work contracts. Again, a percentage of such deals went traditionally to the party war chests. Members of other parties, particularly the Radicals, feared that the Christian Democrats had captured still another means of financing their political campaigns. To the extent that the Christian Democrats' possibilities for obtaining such money increased, the possibilities of the other parties diminished—regardless of whether the Christian Democrats availed themselves of their opportunities.

Although the Radicals agreed with many aspects of Frei's copper program, it was for such interior reasons that they felt bound to make trouble for him. One senator, Luis Bossay, openly admitted that his party's resistance was prompted, in large part, by fears that the Christian Democrats would become a one-party dictatorship. With the stunning Christian Democratic victory in the March 1965 congressional elections, these political fears were polarized. Never before had there been such an overpowering force in Congress. Always before compromise and coalition had been tools of the lawmakers. Now minority-party congressmen hardly knew what to expect. They fought, not against programs or in defense of ideas, but to assert themselves.

The leaders of FRAP were more than disappointed by the defeat. They were angry. They believed they had lost because of wildly exaggerated appeals to fear of communism—as they may very well have. Two American professors, Federico G. Gil of the University of North Carolina and Charles J. Parrish of the University of Texas, made an in-depth analysis of the election and its aftermath. They reported:

> Many voters were so frightened before the election that they laid in a week's supply of food in case of riots or other political upsets that might be attendant on a FRAP victory. Another indication of this anxiety was the fact that airline reservations were booked out of Chile for several months after the elections as a hedge against a FRAP victory. When people are prepared to leave their country because they have supported a losing political candidate, it is safe to say that they are indeed alarmed.

Not only non-Communists within the FRAP, but many leftist intellectuals as well, had taken the anti-Communist effort as an affront, and they vowed to make life for Frei as difficult as possible in the months to come. Frei accepted these confrontations as a great challenge to his administration. For the last four decades, Chilean presidents had seen their programs thwarted by coalitions of minority parties. A nation so desperately in need of social change could no longer bear such obstruction.

The Frei government would need to move swiftly, yet

delicately. It would need to stimulate sluggish economic areas through judicious pressure that would not isolate or alienate the private sector. It would need to convince the private sector that it could produce and profit without fear of nationalization, provided it performed in a manner conducive to the public good. Nor could this problem be solved simply with reassurances. Chile's capitalists, who styled themselves along nineteenth-century laissez-faire lines, would have to be taught some basic contemporary ideas: that for the capitalist to prosper, the people must have purchasing power; that each capitalist must contribute to this power through an enlightened wage policy; that the reinvestment of profits, while theoretically an option, was actually an obligation, for otherwise the country could not grow; that while the capitalist might be content to operate on a modest scale in the shelter of a protected market of low wages and high markups, such a policy could destroy his society; that as a Chilean, he must expand his enterprise in order to provide more jobs, more purchasing power, more taxes. Left alone, the Chilean capitalist would not change. He would have to be taught, perhaps compelled, even coerced. He would have to pay penalties for inaction, such as a tax on what he might have produced, rather than on what he actually produced.

In almost every area of society it was custom and habit that the government would need to attack. The dilettante landowner must plow his fields. The haphazard taxpayer must pay his share. The schoolteacher must revise his course. The bureaucrat must change his rules. The government must dig deeply into the gears of social function and retool. It would not be easy. For example, the government's accounting system provided that the books of all departments must ultimately pass through the hands of one man. Review had become interminable and frustrating. Experts suggested to the chief controller that the procedure be decentralized. "The idea is sensible," he replied, "but the law says I review all accounting, and I shall." Nor was the will for change enough. The ideas would have to be good—a variable factor in the most advanced of countries. Ten months after Frei took office, the well-meaning chief of customs at Los Cerrillos Airport decided to modernize the inspection of incoming baggage. In the past, passengers had waved their declarations at the inspectors as soon as their baggage had been collected; the inspectors would select passengers at random. It was a capricious, disorderly system. Now, the chief decided, inspectors would collect all the declarations, divide them among themselves, and work with their assigned parties. There were two things wrong with the idea. The first was that the inspectors pronounced the names of foreign tourists in an all but unrecognizable manner. The second was that the first man in might be the last one out.

The overriding task for Eduardo Frei was more difficult than changing habits and customs. To succeed, he would need to inspire belief. He would need to convince the people of Chile that they could find themselves. His time limit: until 1970. Should he fail, the Marxists' chances in the next presidential election would be greatly enhanced. It was true that Frei had won 56 percent of the 1964 vote; but almost one million Chileans—38.9 percent of those voting—had been willing to accept a Marxist state. Unquestionably, part of the pivotal vote had been provided by those independents who were willing to give the Christian Democrats a try—and who made no secret of how they would vote the next time should that try fail.

"The problems of Latin America are not Fidel Castro,"

Frei once told a U.S. reporter. "The real problems which must be dealt with are misery, ignorance and poverty. Ignoring these ends is to invite communism to enter, whether from Cuba or elsewhere."

For the North American, such a statement evokes concern. But the concern is academic, the problem inanimate. Only when the American touches Chilean soil does the equation of human endeavors gain life. In every man he can see its factors. Hope multiplied by Possibility equals X. And X becomes Success or Failure, according to the positive or negative characteristic of the factors. In the beginning Hope is positive; Possibility is the only variable. I think of a little boy at Los Cerrillos Airport in Santiago on an August day in 1965 as I arrived from New York to see President Frei. I had cleared customs and hailed a cab, and the driver was stowing my luggage. Out from the crowd darted the boy. He was ten, perhaps twelve, conceivably fourteen; malnourishment makes age hard to figure. He was wearing someone's discarded coat, one sleeve of which was badly ripped. His black hair, badly in need of cutting, kept falling into his eyes. His handsome face was as intent as a dog's at feeding; his manner, as he grabbed for my typewriter, was deft and intrusive. I knew that I had no Chilean money, and no U.S. coins, and so I told him that I did not need his help. But he kept wrestling for my nine-pound typewriter as though this marginal service would somehow validate his life. As I got into the taxi, I told him, "*No tengo plata chilena.*" He would not hear me. In a last desperate gesture, he reached his little hand inside the window and locked the taxi door.

He broke my heart, but he brought me quickly back to Chile.

7

Chile Under Frei

By then, the winds of change had swelled the sea. One remembered Captain Bligh in the Cape of Good Hope, probing the timeless storm on a ceaseless tack. To sail an aged ship of state to fresh waters seemed no less forbidding. The storm breaks. The ship creaks. The crew moans.

"This administration is naïve," protests the industrialist. "It has no political preparation. It's romantic." He is a greying, handsome man, his face, even in winter, dark from rounds of golf. His form is draped in soft flannels cut in the United States. His office is spacious, the furnishings rich but restrained. "They are all politicians of the Left," he continues. "They have an 1850 leftist-mentality. They nationalize, and they don't know whether it's good or bad. Political science here is not good. The trouble is in the universities. There is a lack of maturity of public thinking. They think in slogans. Frei is not sure of himself. He is not delegating authority to others. No one is making decisions.

Ministers lack experience. They wait for Frei, and he for them."

"We've all felt we had a finger in the pie," the bearded young novelist explains. "Everyone had the feeling that he was doing something direct. Everyone knew a senator, or was the cousin of a judge. Everyone was near power; power was a personal thing. Now power is getting to be very abstract. Power has turned out to be a supermarket business. Before it used to be the corner grocery."

A blue Saturday morning. The skier propels his Land Rover toward *Farellones*. Normally it is a two-hour ascent to the slopes from Santiago, but as he storms the mountain it is but ninety minutes. The road narrows, ruts, boomerangs. No matter—he drives like a bullfighter, teasing destiny. The object, he explains, is to pass all others mounting the dirt road, so that they, not you, will eat the dust. The skier and his beautiful daughter beside him are completely relaxed. But their American guest is pushing a foot through the floorboard. Observing his tension, the skier smiles. "Don't suffer," he counsels.

He had emigrated from Spain before World War II, and prospered. But now he is disgusted. A manufacturer, he is cutting back, dropping workers, cursing the Establishment for its egocentricity and lack of ambition, and Chile for its hopeless future. "When the European countries that promised Frei assistance come to Chile and see what it's like—the lack of capital, or market, the taxes, the sense of frustration—you'll see what will happen to their promises to help Chile. No one sees a future here. For a future, they leave the country. It's very agreeable here, a very good life, but Chile will never be anything. We have no middle. We have good generals, good thinkers, the best programs and plans. But right under this we have nothing. All the middleman wants is a job with the government, security for life. And once he gets it, he doesn't perform—and the plans for the country die."

Up he climbs, into the snow. Now the *refugios* of Farellones and La Parva come in view, their rustic frames jutting from rocky ledges. After skiing the wealthy owners will build a fire, sip their drinks and watch the lights come on in the valley below.

"I hope they never pave the road," the skier's daughter says. "When they do, everybody will come, and the place will be spoiled."

"*Egoísmo*," her father chides.

Slowly, barely, almost imperceptibly, Chile was changing. And change was hurting. A tourist might consume a steak-and-wine Sunday dinner at El Parron for $2.35, including tip, and wonder what all the complaints were about. But his dollars would have been sold to a friend ("As a favor, of course") for more than the official rate. The real price of the meal was $3.50, which few Chileans could now afford. Always on Sundays El Parron had been jammed; now, you could count the people.

The government was in a death fight with inflation, and austerity had come to Chile. Imports had been throttled; Scotch whiskey now sold at $25 a fifth. Even the rich were drinking *pisco*. At great political sacrifice the government had frozen further hiring at existing agencies (although it had had to staff new agencies). The country's present

400,000 government employees worried about their jobs. So many had put so much pressure on deputies and senators that the government's program to streamline the bureaucracy was in serious trouble. To quiet the fears, the president himself had recently sent a long explanation to Congress, his anxious plea for understanding undisguised by the cumbersome official language:

> Special care has been taken to disperse any doubt, with interest or with foundation, that could arise from the various sectors which form our public opinion, with reference to the intentions and purposes which inspire the organic modifications and rationalization of the internal government service and public administration, and it has even been established that no public official is going to be lowered in grade, nor will he have his salary diminished . . . The facilities that in this respect are asked by the government, constitute means to put to effect the measures that are required, but with clear limitations, such as it will not signify loss of personnel nor lowering of their salaries; on the contrary, it will mean the coordination of services and functions, with benefits for the public employees, the efficient running of the country, the state and all society.

In the big offices, over gleaming tables at the *Club de la Unión*, in the corridors of the Senate, the members of the Establishment talked of how they might frustrate, and ultimately tame, the new president. Once before, in the 1920's, their fathers had tamed a reformist president. There was no reason they could not do so now. They would hold back their resources. They would ally with the extreme Left. Neither the FRAP nor the Right liked many of Frei's ideas. No matter that they did not agree on why; it only mattered that they both disapproved.

Back and forth, against these winds, tacked the Chilean ship of state. But her captain was not alarmed.

I had last seen Frei in the spring of 1964, when he was

one of three Chilean senators battling for the presidency. Now he was the president, the talk of Latin America, the symbol of a new and hopeful order. Then I had gone to Frei's office with Gardner Cowles to pick him up for lunch; he had taken my hand and pulled me to him for an earnest *abrazo*. Now, as I walked through the curtained entrance to the president's office, Frei once again pulled me to him for a sustained Latin greeting, "So glad to see you," he said in Spanish, and the pressure on my ribs convinced me that he was. Immediately, he asked for my wife, Jacquelyn, who was to have come to Santiago with me, but who had sprained her back a few weeks earlier. She was better, I told him, but still held to her bed. He said her problem was very common in Chile.

And then we got to work. I told Frei that what had started as a book about him had become as much a book about Chile and Chileans. To speak of a president, you must speak of his problems. To speak of his problems, you must speak of history and geography and institutions, of success and failure. Thus, a president can only be seen against the background of his country. On the chance that Frei's ego might be ruffled, I had been somewhat apprehensive about this announcement. But he was relieved.

I had countless questions, I told him. For many of the answers I would see party members, government officials, professors, diplomats. Ultimately, I told him, I would want to discuss each point with him. I would need many hours. Frei strode to his desk and rang a bell. His aide-de-camp, Colonel Felix Guerrero Salcedo, appeared immediately. Frei instructed Guerrero to block out large chunks of time for each weekday that I would be in Chile. The colonel nodded, and disappeared. Frei turned to me. "Can we start?" I asked. *"Fuego!"* said Frei.

Mindful of the difficulties and contradictions that had

developed since his inauguration, I asked Frei whether his understanding of the presidency had changed since he took office.

Frei smiled. The answer, he said, was paradoxical. In certain ways he was more optimistic than he had been; in others, more pessimistic. "Why am I optimistic?" he asked aloud. He began to pace, then stopped abruptly and turned to me. "I am going to answer you straight," he said. "If a Chilean journalist asked the same question, I would tell him that everything is wonderful. For you, I must go into the interior of my thought.

"In what way am I optimistic?" he asked again. "I believe the people are much more concerned and involved, have a much greater sense of the possibilities and are more realistic than I had hoped. An example: I thought the people would press for wage increases, but they haven't. The people are sincerely against the inflation; they are the real anti-*inflacionistas*. They seem to understand that we must have a pause in order to regroup and gain strength. They are willing to wait.

"My second reason for optimism: This country has much greater resources, human as well as economic, than I had dared hope. Wherever you invest your resources, the response is twenty times greater than I had anticipated.

"The negative factors: In political circles, very negative. The politicians are preoccupied with the little things, the party things, the egoistic things. The political by-play doesn't correspond to the generosity of the people. For the Communists, all that counts is their strategy against the U.S. They don't care about improving the country. Oh, they care, but it's secondary."

I asked why that would surprise him. He answered, "There's an old proverb: 'We all know we're going to die, but we don't really believe it.' "

His second disappointment, Frei said, was the administrative inertia he had discovered. "From afar, I hadn't seen the deficiency with clarity. There are the generals, the thinkers, and then there are the mass of the people. But in-between there are not enough technicians to execute the ideas. There are not enough doers. A great deficiency."

His third disappointment, Frei said, had been on the international level, where he had found the other Latin American countries indecisive about forming a Latin American union. On the whole, however, his feelings inclined to be positive. He had been overwhelmed by the reaction everywhere to his election, and by the good will of others toward him.

And so began eight days of conversations with the president of Chile.

We would meet each afternoon in his office overlooking the square. We would sit in deep chairs of dark brown leather, but the moment I asked a question Frei would bolt from his seat and pace across the green carpet, passing countless times under a great gold chandelier hanging from the ceiling twenty feet above. After each of my questions, his brow would crease; he would put a hand to his head, or stare vacantly, or inspect the floor. Then he would begin a long but systematic answer, underscored occasionally with anger. Only rarely would we be interrupted by a priority call, but each crisis would have to wait until the president of Chile, as if in some comic movie, had picked up several of his telephones until he had found the right one.

This was a time for crises in Chile. Frei's opponents in Congress were forming alliances to defeat his copper bill. The private sector was all but inert. Some industrialists were succumbing with incongruous ease to demands by union leaders, most of them FRAP supporters, for wages that exceeded the ceiling set by Frei. For all Frei's problems, however, I once again had that sense of communion with him; except for the rare calls, his attention never wavered.

We would talk for a while in his office, and then move through the palace to the baronial dining hall. There, at a table set for fourteen, we two would sit to tea. Everything about the room was immense—the proportions, the chandelier, the dark mahogany table with five large, widely-spaced chairs to a side and two at each end, even the poor mural of a *conquistador* at the far end of the room.

Tea in Chile is the third of four meals, a bridge between lunch at 1 P.M. and dinner at 10 P.M. it consists of toast, little sandwiches, cakes, fruit and beverages. Frei would begin with a sweet, thick, milky fruit drink, eat some buttered toast, sip his tea, then bound from the table to pace the glistening floor, now declaiming from a distant corner, now pounding his two big fists down the length of the table. And I would sit in a big armchair, furiously making notes, unable even to sip the tea. At one point, my preoccupation so disturbed Frei that he stopped in mid-sentence. "I like you to look at me when we talk," he complained. "Why won't you let my secretary take notes?" Frei had made the same offer on our first day together; I had accepted reluctantly, because it had been my experience that verbatim transcription tends to inhibit most people. The first transcript had borne me out; Frei had been more constrained than usual. I had then requested that we work alone, and he had acceded. Now, however, Frei was responding so totally that I felt the danger had passed. I agreed.

We covered many subjects in our days together, yet two persistent themes unified our dialogue. The first was the

failure of the existing Chilean social organization to provide the average Chilean with a confirming life. The second was the delicate scoring that would be required to
harmonize the new and old orders. The new might easily
overwhelm the old, much as ponderous brasses might out-
play more delicate strings.

The first theme has found its proper place elsewhere in
this book. Here, I wish to emphasize the second. It is in my
estimation, and I believe in Frei's, his crucial problem, for
it goes to the root of social organization. If Frei cannot
marshal the private sector, he will not only fail to achieve
the society he projects, he will be forced to a type of socialism he neither advocates nor desires.

Frei has a considerable appreciation of the limitations of
state enterprise—its propensity to fat, sloth, deficit. But
history has demonstrated, he believes, that Chilean private
enterprise will not properly develop certain economic
areas, and will not even venture into others. In these cases,
he has concluded, the government has no alternative but to
engage itself.

The government's long-range objective is to educate the
private sector to an altogether new appreciation of its obligations to society. But before the government can hope to
do that, it must first convince the private sector that it can
and should commit itself to investment in Chile under a
mildly socialist regime. At the moment, critical elements of
the private sector reserve their resources in anticipation of
some positive sign that they will be permitted to operate to
their profit.

Frei's closest economic advisors believe that the administration must spell out to private enterprise exactly where
its functions lie. The government should specify which sectors it intends to operate (for example, gas, electricity, and

basic industries), which it intends to share with private enterprise (including copper and cement), and which sectors would be open exclusively to private enterprise. In addition, the advisors believe the entrepreneurs might be encouraged if they knew specifically what their increased tax obligations would be during the remaining years of the Frei administrations. Uncertainty would be eliminated, and the entrepreneurs could make mature projections.

Frei sympathizes with the entrepreneurs and would like to encourage them. But he believes that the problem is more profound than they imagine, and cannot be solved simply by setting forth the ground rules.

"We are interested in an effective development of the private sector," he insists. "We desire its co-operation, and we want to establish solid bases for its development. The first base is to terminate the inflation. With a big inflation, all development is impossible. In order to terminate the inflation, it's necessary to correct errors of both the state and the private sector. It's easy to do this when one has right and the other has wrong. What's difficult is when both have a certain amount of right."

He offers the price of milk, which the government controls, as an example. When Frei took office, the price was very low. He promptly raised it. "Never has milk had a greater price increase than this year. But here we see clearly how complicated the problem is. The grower cannot produce at this price, and the consumer cannot pay a higher price. It does nothing to permit a great increase in the price of milk if the salaried people cannot buy it. If I price milk at 500 pesos, and the great mass of Chileans have a salary of more or less 2000 pesos (a day), 25 percent of a man's salary would go for one litre of milk. I have to go by steps, and try to improve both their situations."

140

The worker should receive a better salary, and the farmer should have a more economically sound operation. "Farmers are leaving the milk business because the price of milk has made its production very unattractive to them. Other lands would be more suitable for dairies, but in order to develop them, I have to have refrigerated cars to transport the milk. I must also streamline the production of milk. I can't resolve these problems in a year. But that's not because I don't see the problem."

Several fundamental questions emerge from this example. Did the dairymen ever study new farming methods? Did they reinvest their profits, during years of prosperity? Might increased investment, plus modern technology, have enabled them to lower their unit cost? Could they, by advertising, have enlarged the size of their market? "We do not have the type of businessmen who go out and create markets," one government economist observes sadly. "They wait first for demand, and only then produce."

Frei understands acutely the subjective factor involved in successful capitalism. "We admire capitalism as it has worked in the U.S. But it hasn't worked for us," he remarked once. The point is crucial. To Frei, the private sector is useful to Chile to the extent that it serves the people. It frequently fails to do so. For example, certain Chilean industrialists obstruct government attempts to arrest inflation. Instead of heeding the government's mandate to limit wages to a 20 percent increase, the employers accede readily to union demands for as much as 40 percent. Are the employers being generous? Hardly. The increase gives them an excuse to raise their own prices, thereby provoking the inflationary spiral they have learned to use to their profit—expanding on borrowed money that is half its value or less by the time they pay it back.

141

When private enterprise acts against the interests of the people, the government must intervene, says Frei. He has little patience for those who at that point cry out, "Socialism."

"Here," Frei offered once, "Chile imports light fixtures. So a man comes to you and he says, 'Mr. President, I would like to go into the production of light fixtures, so that Chile doesn't have to import them.' And you tell him that this is an excellent idea for Chile. And then he says, 'But if I'm to produce light fixtures, Mr. President, you must put up a tariff wall to protect me against imports from the U.S. and France and Japan.' And so you put up a tariff barrier for him. And what happens? One, maybe two companies begin to produce light fixtures. And they make an agreement between them to control the supply and the price of light fixtures. And they don't care about efficiency, or quality, because they have a monopoly on light fixtures. And they charge a very high price for a very poor product. So who pays for the light fixtures? The people. Then you, the government, decide that you must control the price of light fixtures. And the moment you do that, the light-fixture manufacturer cries, 'Socialism!'" The president leaned forward, his hand opened like a supplicant's. "Socialism is government intervention. But who was it who first asked the government to intervene? The manufacturer of light fixtures."

Frei believes that the whole pattern of capitalist conduct in Chile indicates that the private sector must be restructured before it can be expected to perform adequately. His is the extraordinarily difficult job of remodeling without destroying. How he proposes to accomplish this task is seen best in his agrarian reform measure.

In essence, the reform recognizes the right of private

property, yet provides for expropriation where property is not used productively. Under the measure, subsistence farming by land speculators is not sufficient to hold onto property. Poorly worked property is also vulnerable. The reform measure elaborates with great care what constitutes poorly worked property—more than thirty-seven basic irrigation acres, 80 percent of whose irrigated sections and 70 percent of whose dry sections are not gainfully utilized; or 50 percent of whose overall area is not treated with fertilizer. The owner of such property must also have made investments equal to the value of the unimproved land. Abnormally large tracts are also subject to expropriation.

An owner can avoid expropriation in a number of ways, but basically, all he would need to do was prove to the government that he either planned or was executing a program to develop his property. An owner also has the right to reserve two hundred acres for himself, and should he have more than five children, a smaller amount of land for each of his children in excess of five. In this case, the owner must exploit the land satisfactorily himself.

The agrarian reform measure also strikes at another fundamental of Chilean society—the tradition of "water rights." Such rights, ceded initially to the first *conquistadores*, have passed from generation to generation. The man who possessed such rights not only had the most prosperous land, he was privileged to charge others whatever he wished for the use of the water. Under the government's reform measure, water rights are deemed "national property for public use."

Expropriated lands would be paid for in government bonds, which would bear interest of 3 percent on the face amount, plus 50 percent of an adjusted value to be determined each year according to the change in the official wholesale price index. The payment itself would be based on the valuation for tax purposes.

The last matter, of course, was the blockbuster. Land-owners have always placed a ridiculously low value on their property, and now they were suddenly confronted with the possibility that they would be paid a ridiculously low sum for it. The ironic justice of the proposal left them unimpressed.

Perhaps the most radical departure from tradition of the measure is that expropriated property can be occupied immediately by the government, regardless of whether the payment has been agreed upon or made. This, says Frei, constitutes the essence of the reform. In years past, owners have always been able to stave off action by appeals to various courts including the Supreme Court. Since the legal process in Chile is even more time-consuming than in the United States, the effect has been to preclude any kind of agrarian reform.

Critics of the measure say it amounts to outright confiscation. Frei emphatically disagrees. "If I expropriate your property I have to pay you money. If you're not satisfied, you can begin a judicial process to establish the real value." He compared the old and new systems. "You have a *fundo* and it's put into agrarian reform. And I say to you, 'This *fundo* is worth a thousand million pesos and I will pay you this amount.' But you say, 'I'm not of accord. My *fundo* is worth two thousand million pesos, and I desire to name a commission to fix the price.' Then commences the process to establish its true value. I am not able to touch your property, and finally, when they define how much the value of the property has risen I must give you a check, and you give me charge of the property. That's what happens today. What is the reform I propose? I say to you, 'Sir, you have a *fundo* that has a value of a thousand million pesos. I declare expropriation.' To you this seems bad, so you go to the tribune. But meanwhile, the state is already in charge of the *fundo*. If at the end of the year it is necessary to pay you fifteen hundred millions, okay, we will pay. But meanwhile we are working. This is the difference. But you always have the right to go to the tribune."

Can Frei achieve such structural modifications? In August 1965 he was optimistic. "I believe my country will realize the changes," he said then. "We are in a very good condition to realize them. I believe I'm going to do it. I believe I have the capacity. Maybe there will be a political problem, but if there is no obstacle, I can do it."

Problem after problem arose during the next few months. The Establishment, fearing an attack on the concept of private property, defended it at every step—even if defense required an alliance with the Marxists. The Establishment's main battleground became the Chilean Senate, where the confluence of far Right and far Left at the point of opposition was enough, for the moment, to frustrate Frei.

By January 1966 (a year after it was first proposed), Frei's legislative cornerstone, the program to "Chileanize" American-owned copper mines through separate partnership deals between Anaconda, Kennecott, the Cerro Corporation and the Chilean government, had been badly disfigured. Opposition had come from leftist Radicals, Socialists and Communists, who believed that Frei was consigning national resources to the foreigners. But the obstructionists also included conservatives, who feared that the principle of "Chileanization," if established in the copper bill, would lead to other reforms—including land reform. Together the opponents were able to eliminate guarantee provisions—without which partnership arrangements with Kennecott and Cerro could not go forward.

There were other signs of trouble. Copper miners, in a move largely interpreted as designed to embarrass Frei and protest his agreement with the U.S. companies, struck for higher wages, insisting that Frei had promised the workers a share in profits. The government, which badly wants friendship with labor, vacillated. Finally, it capitulated to the strikers; it not only met their demands, it paid them for the time they had struck. And the successful strike provoked others. To at least one competent observer, the strategy of the radical Left was plain: "When Marxism loses a political battle, it goes on the trade union front. That's elementary tactics." An election of officers in the Chilean trade union confederation resulted in victories for Communists and Socialists, but not one Christian Democrat.

One party leader blamed the poor result on the failure of the party's labor department to obtain adequate procedural guarantees from the Marxist groups controlling the mechanisms of the Congress in the months prior to the meeting. By the time the assurances were offered, it was too late for the Christian Democrats to mobilize their strength. However valid the explanation may be, the fact is that the Christian Democrats have been much weaker than they would like to be in their political work with the unions. An angry critic said:

> Frei has done nothing that's at the heart of his message— to involve the people. He could have vitalized intermediate groups—organizing the 90 percent of the Chilean work force

that isn't organized, dynamizing the state and municipal governments by involvement of the people, creating savings and loan associations, and so on. He hasn't done anything in this field. Do you think Lenin would have started his revolution by worrying about a copper bill?

Many of Chile's liberals grumbled. "Nothing major has happened," said an architect. "A few bills, but nothing major. We need structural change. If Frei doesn't get it . . . well, I've supported him every time—when he ran for senator I supported him, I supported him for the presidency—but if he doesn't get it done, I'll vote Socialist the next time. We'll all vote Socialist."

To others, however, the Christian Democrats had hurt their cause *because* of their efforts, some of which the critics considered ill-prepared. "They want too much in their first years," one diplomat remarked. "They will be judged over six years, but they don't see this. The risks of failure of too crash a program are very great." Said another critic: "Some Christian Democrats tend to be ridiculous, egocentric. They overtheorize about Christianism and the Church. They extrapolate from the encyclicals. They lack experience; they have nonsensical ideas. They desire to be the leader of Latin America before they have shown their capability of running Chile. I think the Chileans have oversold themselves."

For anyone inclined to be pessimistic about Frei's chances of implementing his program, there are examples available, therefore. But for the optimists there was excellent material too.

There is a mechanistic way of gauging political progress. One could say that in its first year in office, the Frei government cut the rate of inflation from 38 percent to 25 percent; that domestic spending dropped, as did nonessential imports; that Chile's internal debt fell remarkably, from $133.3 million to $78.6 million, and its foreign debt rose only slightly, from $1,834,000,000 to $1,986,000,000. Foreign creditors, impressed, agreed to refinance $500 million of maturing debt. Lending shriveled. As the reins of austerity tightened, commerce constricted so much that the government had to let up somewhat. Even so, the effect of all the efforts was to bring Chile within sight of price stability by 1968. The significance of such a feat could not be exaggerated. Said one observer: "If they reverse the course of inflation, it will show that the Christian Democrats have not only the intent, but the ability to run the country."

And the president did get his copper bill at last—and in a manner as significant as the new law itself. Rebuffed on key provisions of the bill as it was first passed by Congress in January, Frei turned swiftly to a new tack. The Chamber of Deputies had passed a wage readjustment bill, which included a rider containing the critical guarantee provisions the FRAP-Radical-Conservative-Liberal opposition had blocked on the copper bill's initial passage. If Frei could corner one-third plus one of the Senate vote, he could under Chilean law block Senate disapproval of the lower chamber's bill. Victory would then be his.

But he would need more than his own thirteen Christian Democratic senators. To obtain the necessary votes, he turned to the Liberals and Conservatives in the Senate.

Now these men made their real interests clear. Their passion was reserved not for copper but for land. The copper agreement simply furnished them with a perfect bargaining point in their attempt to modify the government's proposed agrarian reform law. The traditionalists had agreed some months before to the principle of agrarian reform; what they were seeking now, in exchange for their support on the copper bill, were guarantees relating to property rights.

For weeks Frei and his lieutenants pressed the Conservatives and Liberals, but as of March 30 (one day before the vote on the copper amendments) the administration did not have the votes. That day, in a lengthy meeting, government forces agreed to give "honest and serious consideration" to new suggestions of the Liberals and Conservatives; they pointed out that the government had already accepted more than fifty "perfecting" suggestions made by farm owners and conservative congressional elements. The legislators listened, and remained noncommital.

The evening of March 31, Frei returned to his home at 9:30, worn from another day of incessant pleading. At 10 P.M. he received a telephone call from his minister of justice. Five Conservative and Liberal party leaders had asked to see him at once. Congress was still in session, with the vote on the copper amendments now only hours away.

Frei received the men. Their spokesman, Francisco Bulnes, a Conservative senator, told the president that they would support his bill if he would modify the method of determining property values for purposes of compensation under the proposed agrarian reform law.

At this point the Latin in the president conquered the Swiss. Incensed, Frei curtly refused. He denounced the men for their last-minute attempt to hold up his program. He reminded his callers that they had agreed to the same compensation provision in an earlier law enacted under the Alessandri administration; he said he would not trade on the principle of agrarian reform. As an opposition senator he had supported government bills that he considered worthy; since his callers admitted the copper bill was worthy, they were morally obligated to support it. What angered him most, the president told his listeners, was that in months of discussions with his administration on agrarian reform, including the protracted discussion of the day before, they had never once raised the compensation issue. He found their timing obvious and distasteful, and their strategy futile.

There was no purpose to be served in further discussions the president said. But before his guests left, he wanted to tell them a few things. His gaze withering, Frei then verbally lashed his callers. They were, he said, being unfaithful to their office by such crass bargaining for gain. Furthermore, they were playing with fire. Should his government fail, their own predicament in 1970 would be far worse. They might be able to talk to a Christian Democratic government, he pointed out, but they would be denied this privilege under a Marxist government. His patience, the president said, was not without limits. It could one day give way. He had agreed to many changes in the agrarian reform proposals, he said, but should the men continue to act in this fashion, he could and would push the bill through in a form far less acceptable to them.

The effect of Frei's lecture was remarkable—and historic. One by one the callers began to reassure each other that the copper bill, and the government, really did deserve their support. They said good night and drove back to the Senate, where, just before midnight, the crucial agreements passed their last legislative hurdle—with the support of the Conservative and Liberal parties.

Although the copper bill was an elaborate piece of legislation its essence was quite simple. Basically, it was an attempt by the government to involve itself in exploiting Chilean resources to a degree never before accomplished. Through partnerships with the U.S. copper companies, Frei hoped to double production. The inducement for the U.S. companies was a greatly reduced rate of taxation.

The legislation passed in the early morning hours of April 1 still failed to deal with the problems involved in the transfer of Kennecott Copper Corporation's Braden properties to a new Chilean corporation, but both the Anaconda Company and the Cerro Corporation could now proceed with their expansion plans. Hopes for a settlement of the Kennecott problems were high.

But the details were secondary. The primary consideration was the scope and intent of the plan. As the *New York Times* pointed out in an editorial extolling the development: "Three companies alone—Braden with $200 million, Anaconda with $150 million and Cerro with about $85 million—plan to invest nearly half as much as the United States puts into the Alliance for Progress in a year." The *Times* went on: ". . . . One result should be a greatly increased national income in Chile to finance the Government's proposed agrarian reform. . . . By August of this year President Frei's program should get moving, and it is conceivable that an era of prosperity for Chile will begin."

True, there were grave problems with Marxist-dominated unions, so serious they culminated in a violent battle between striking mine workers and soldiers in March 1966. But the origin and aftermath of that battle bear careful scrutiny. Early in 1966, some 10,000 workers at the Braden Copper Company's El Teniente mine, frustrated in their attempt to secure wage demands two and one-half times in excess of the legal limit ordered by the

THE LAST, BEST HOPE

government, and probably encouraged by the government's display of weakness in handling an earlier copper strike in November 1965, voted to stop work. The government attempted to mediate the dispute, but otherwise took the position that the strike was legal. However, when workers at mines in the North called for sympathy strikes of twenty-four and forty-eight hours, the government, mindful of its error the previous fall, reacted with firmness. It declared the new strikes illegal and ordered work to be resumed. Most of the strikers obeyed. But at one northern mine, resistance developed. For one day workers at Anaconda's El Salvador mine succeeded in a 100 percent work stoppage. On the second day 70 percent of the workers heeded the government's order to return to work; the remaining 30 percent, urged on by their union, tried to stop them. At this point the armed forces commander in the area declared a state of emergency and forbade the union to hold a protest meeting. It was held nonetheless. The commander then sent troops to break it up. Workers fired revolvers at the troops, wounding their captain; the soldiers returned the fire. Eight miners were killed, and thirty-five wounded.

The events that followed could affect Chile's political life for years. Frei was to have traveled to Talca, a city south of Santiago, to make a speech; the El Salvador incident had forced him to cancel the trip. But a newspaper report from Talca that an attempt would be made on his life caused him to reverse his plans again. The next morning he flew to Talca, to be greeted by an emotional reception from 20,000 Chileans chanting, *"No afloje, Presidente, el pueblo está presente."* ("Don't give way, Mr. President, the people are here.") In Santiago the high command of FRAP called for a nation-wide general strike. The day before the general strike, *pobladores* from the slums, house-wives and students jammed the spacious Constitution Plaza in front of *La Moneda* to cheer the embattled president. Many were motivated by an explosive new factor. In the wake of the shooting at El Salvador, Fidel Castro had broadcast a vicious attack on Frei, calling him " . . . a reactionary, vulgar politician . . . a coward [who had] promised revolution without blood but has given only blood without revolution." The general strike the next day was a fiasco; only 35,000 out of a total labor force of 3 million stayed away from their jobs. A brief footnote to the whole episode was that the striking workers ended their eighty-seven day walkout on April 1—the day the government won its great legislative victory—and for the 25 percent increase the government had been urging them to accept all along.

The assessment of progress in Chile depended on which men you saw. Many entrepreneurs lacked confidence in the government and were holding back on investments. But others were beginning to reconcile themselves to the new state of affairs. "There's a feeling on the part of Chilean businessmen that it's time to come into the twentieth century," a development expert just back from the country insisted. *El Mercurio*, the country's leading newspaper, reported proudly that Chile could now produce all the synchronization elements needed for traffic signals. In his cavernous dining room, the newspaper's publisher, young Augustin E. Edwards III, was so preoccupied in discussing plans for expansion that his luncheon plate was served and removed without being touched. "I'm a fool," he said. "I'm putting everything I have into the land." The private sector will ultimately take its risks, he predicted. "It's got to reinvest in order to stay in business."

One firm sign of change was the election of Luis Larraín, an enlightened young man, as president of the hoary *Sociedad Nacional de Agricultura* in 1965. Under Larraín, the SNA began meaningful discussions with the government on land reform problems, and in January 1966, signed its first contracts with democratic farm unions.

The ambitious program the Christian Democrats had set for themselves encouraged some observers. Said one, "I found a sense of political leadership I'd never felt before. There was a tremendous sense of euphoria for the direction the party had taken." Another remarked: "You never reach the question of their commitment, their belief in economic growth and the distribution of that growth to the society. There is a horrible distribution-of-income problem here. Their complete conviction on this point is impressive. In the Alessandri administration, only with certain officials did you get a sense of their sincerity. They didn't basically believe in any of the tenets of the Alliance for Progress. They were playing games. The idea of distribution didn't exist. You had the feeling they were saying things about land reform and tax reform because they thought that American officials wanted to hear it. They responded to the extent of their need to respond, rather than to their internal conviction. There was a constant political appeal made to you in the former administration. The conservatives would say, 'You have no alternative. Your future is with us.' They'd give you the 'threat-of-Allende' argument. The new administration sticks to the problems."

Its directness gave a no-nonsense quality to the Frei government—particularly in that most crucial of matters, the individual's financial support. "People with money are now conscious that they're facing an administration that doesn't countenance tax evasion. They have made credible the idea that people who evade are going to suffer." Collections in the first half of 1965 were up 24 percent over the same period the previous year. One Chilean was in jail for tax fraud—the first time anyone had been imprisoned for this offense in the country's history. When Congress passed a tax-forgiveness law—permitting anyone who paid his back taxes within sixty days to go unpunished—Frei vetoed the bill with a harsh message against favoritism. When a congressional committee resisted an administration proposal for enforcing provisions against tax evasion, a government minister, Sergio Molina, threatened to make public a list of the taxes that committee members themselves were paying. He got almost everything he wanted, including a capital tax on assets.

Casting about for ways to raise efficiency and conserve electricity, the government surveyed a sample of Chilean workers, and found that 95 percent of them would gladly abandon the traditional three-hour lunch (most of which they spent on crowded buses getting to and from their homes) for a 9 A.M. to 4:30 P.M. working day. The government then decreed the compact day,* and made sure that workers would spend their new free time at home by ordering bars to close between 4 P.M. and 7 P.M.

Slowly, in such varied ways, the administration was conveying a sense of authenticity to the people. Success in making itself credible would be historic. Chileans, with good reason, have never really believed in government. They have seen too many promises broken, too many "plans" unrealized. Cynicism permeates their thinking. "Our people don't have an economic sense; they don't

---

* The measure was later abandoned by retail stores when it was found that the new hours cut deeply into sales.

build for the future; they don't believe the politicians," observes a Chilean experienced in these matters. His one worry is that Frei, to impress and politicize the people, might offer them more social programs than he should at this time. "Frei is sometimes so influenced by politics that he loses sight of what the people want. He is offering a revolution in freedom, but he knows that it will require more than six years. He has been promising more on the social side than he can deliver. This administration is extremely sentimentally involved in housing. But things must be balanced. The party is full of idealism, and doesn't realize how complicated it is to introduce new elements into the society. It would be good in the short range, but it would destroy economic progress in the next few years.

"Frei cannot fail on economics. If he builds houses, schools, roads, but loses on economics, then the Communists will win the next election. Frei's program is fundamentally sound. It basically must push exports. At the same time, there must be enough social elements to prove that you're doing the revolution in freedom—more services at little or no cost. That is the way you redistribute income." But the main effort, says this Chilean, must be to control inflation, stabilize the currency, create a broad economic base that in turn will create more and better jobs. "The people will have confidence in Frei if they see that he is doing the right thing, even if he's not moving at the speed they had wanted. You must be sure that you're building for your children's future. If the people see you are moving in the right direction, they will give you the time."

Chile's problem is not a mechanical one. There are too many excellent mechanics in the world who know how to tinker the engine of change into phase. The problem is that the producing forces do not understand the ratio of their effort to the engine's performance. Says a government economist: "Our prosperity is based on purchasing power. We cannot convince the entrepreneur of this. He must be made to understand."

Frei could (and many wish he would) use the ample powers of the presidency. But those who urge radical acts do not appreciate what an overwrought effort would do. It might set the engine in motion, but at the risk of great internal damage. Like an automobile whose differential has not been packed, the gears are eventually destroyed, and the vehicle ceases to move. Then a new set of gears is required to get it moving again.

Frei would like to work with the gears he has. His problem is to make them mesh. He knows what a good mechanic knows—that this cannot be done with a hammer.

Once, during our discussions, I asked Frei why Chile, which had always nurtured men eager for social justice, had never risen to their call. His answer, I think, does more than explain history; it reveals why he believes he can succeed where others have failed. "They promised more than they could give, or than the people could absorb," he said. "They had no organization, no ideas, no system, no moral structure. They didn't tell the people that what they were talking about had to be achieved in steps. Every failure reinforced the peoples' conviction of fate, of helplessness."

We were in the dining room, I sitting at the right of the president's chair, the president standing across the huge table from me, a good fifteen feet away. Now he began to pace down the length of the table, then along its width. "In these Latin American countries there is an electoral explosion now and then. But there is a social structure. The centers of power are permanent, they keep going." With his two big fists, the president planted "power centers" every few feet atop the table. "They keep going, but the electoral explosion dissipates." Frei paused. "The answer, the way to bust out of this, is that when the government doesn't give justice, you have to push against the centers of power. My way of doing this is *Promoción Popular*. This is the key, the backbone, the center of my whole government."

It is precisely here that the gears would mesh. It is one thing for a politician to aver that government must provide a good life for the people. It is another for him to understand the functional relationship between the welfare of state and people. When Frei says that Chile "will not save itself either by the force of the state or of certain groups, but by the force of the entire people," he conjures up not simply a dream, but an economy agitated by massive injections of purchasing power. When half the society cannot purchase, the other half can produce only half of what it might. The two halves must be joined. Says Frei:

> Only to the extent that this integration makes itself effective will we be able to mobilize the human resources of our country and authenticate our democracy. . . . Our objective consists not only of an economic development, but of a social development, that there may be education, a good life, health, that the increase or riches, gotten with hard work, may be distributed equally. In order to obtain this we cannot follow the path of private paternalism or state paternalism. Everyone must contribute to the community so that all of the forces together can succeed. This incorporation of man into the national community organisms is what we call *Promoción Popular*.
>
> There is no true democracy without an organized people capable of representing themselves in all the sectors that constitute the citizens' life. The right to vote is not enough: The people must have the means to play a role in determining the destiny of their nation. Therefore, *Promoción Popular*

signifies basic community organizations that enable the people to express themselves. This is what characterizes democracy in developed countries—where the power is not encountered in small groups or in the state.

In form, these organizations would be community centers, syndicates and co-operatives. But the essense of "popular promotion" is to bring the individual to some meaningful sense of himself.

Half the population of Chile has received nothing from the country—no gratification, no possibility, not even a neighboring telephone from which to call an ambulance in case of need. Not only have elements of this half of Chile never been present when decisions were made, most of them have never made a meaningful decision in their lives. The substance of *Promoción Popular* is that the act of making a decision is at least as important as the decision itself. The program involves no charity or welfare; it is not even a training program, for it does no good to set up a technical assistance program if the human being involved does not believe he is capable of being trained. What the program does is to provide the setting in which marginal people can organize themselves, represent themselves before public powers and ultimately influence their own destiny. In short, it makes them believe in themselves.

When Frei took office he appointed Sergio Ossa, a forty-seven-year-old engineer and father of seven, to head *Promoción Popular*. Ossa is a deeply religious man who had been "called" by the Catholic Church a few years earlier to start a private development institution. "You have my entire support," Frei told Ossa on his new appointment. "Whatever you say, whatever you do, I say it, I do it." Recalls Ossa: "I have never in my life received such support from a man."

To Ossa, the incorporation of the forgotten half of Chile

into the mainstream is "going to be the deep, deep change in our country. We never forget we are making a revolution *in freedom* for the first time in the world. It will establish the difference between any other government and this one."

Frei, with his strong sense of history, knows that this kind of social reorganization will take years. He is unruffled by critics who would have the program take wing. To Frei, its ultimate flight is inevitable, because the moral force behind it is so powerful. Until recently, such force did not exist in Chile. Today it does, and because it does, the perspective on Frei and his program improves immeasurably.

8

The Deep Change

To an extent it is possible to work up political balance sheets based on tangible assets and liabilities. One credits an electoral triumph, debits the defeat of a bill. But the equation of political progress is arithmetic only to a point. Beyond that, it must be expressed in factors that defy quantitative measure. It is in these intangibles that the deep change in Chile can be found.

Certainly the tangibles are imposing. When a Chilean official speaks of a people able to give a president time to execute his program, he is saying something that no Chilean has ever been able to say before. In political terms "the people" no longer means what it did. True, the Chilean Establishment maintains extraordinary power, particularly through its adroit use of members and momentary allies in the Senate. But against this residual force must be placed another whose potency does not seem to have registered properly on many of those who despair of Frei's—or anyone's—chances of breaking through the encrusted structure of Chilean life. The new factor in Chile's political equation—one that requires all other calculations to be revised—is this: Eduardo Frei was elected by an enormous sector of Chilean society that had never voted before. Between 1958 and 1964 the number of voters in Chile increased by more than it had in all of the thirty previous years combined. This process of democratization is irreversible; the election of Frei reflects the will of a new Chilean majority.

It is conceivable that this new majority will turn in despair to a Marxist solution if Frei's program has not become reality by 1970. It is equally conceivable, however, that the new political group, having voted for reform in a democratic context, will not permit its will to be frustrated for that long by either the radical Left or the conservative Right, or the two combined. Elections for the Senate occur every four years. If the pattern of the last election holds in the next, Frei would have a working majority in the Senate as well as the Chamber of Deputies by 1969, and the last obstacle to effective legislation would be removed.

There are hard political formulas to be figured on the basis of numbers. But the real significance of these numbers is in their emotional force. When the arithmetic dimension of voting is deepened by the geometric dimension of content, the meaning of change in Chile becomes clear.

The historic feature of Frei's election was not simply his victory. Nor was it that in articulating the needs of Chile, he provided a specific program. Frei unleashed a force. He mobilized a latent sense of responsibility among Chileans—particularly among the youth. By American standards the feat may not seem impressive, but by Chilean standards it is extraordinary.

In 1965, several thousand students traveled to the south of Chile during their vacation to build schools, hospitals and other facilities for the poor. The extraordinary size of the group indicated the increasing involvement of the Chilean youth. One explanation was offered by a U.S. State Department specialist in youth affairs on his return late that year from a prolonged inspection trip through Latin America:

> In Chile, as nowhere else in the hemisphere, young people have found a leader in whom they believe, to whom they will look for inspiration and ideals, for whom they are willing to work and sacrifice, and from whom they will accept discipline and authority. They believe that it is possible to get the changes, the reforms, the improvements, the revolution through this man and this movement. There is no other political movement in Latin America today which inspires that kind of hope among its militants other than Mao Tse-tung terrorism.

The specialist pointed out that young Chileans responded to Frei's Christian Democracy for many of the same reasons they had identified with John F. Kennedy's New Frontier. Both embodied historical perspective, intellectual content and emotional appeal. "Frei, like Kennedy, didn't concern himself with the 'how.' He concerned himself with the 'why.' When you live in a country where the consensus is building, the 'why' is an important element of the construction. Just the 'how' is not enough."

If Frei were casting seeds onto barren soil, his efforts would produce no harvest. He is not. The soil is being prepared by new forces, with new tools. Change in Chile is occurring on many levels, in many ways, within institutions as well as within individuals. Some of these changes are not manifestly political, yet all have enormous political implications. What they share in common is the revelation that change itself is possible.

Of all the profound changes underway in Chile, none exceeds those that are taking place within the Roman Catholic Church. Historically the Church has maintained a conservative position. Its failure to apply its ample social doctrine to worldly affairs not only compromised its position with liberal elements in the society, but gravely weakened the country's imperative for change. So closely had the Church been identified in the public mind with the conservative Establishment, that the Christian Democrats prudently took a private sounding during the presidential campaign to determine the political liabilities of any identification the public might make between itself and the Church hierarchy. The results of that poll say a great deal about what has happened to the Church in the last several years. Almost universally, those polled characterized the "old Church" as reactionary. But today, they said, the Chuch is a vigorous force for social reform.

The Church has earned the praise. Its bishops today are without question the most progressive in all Latin America. Their impact is felt all the way to the Vatican Council, where they articulated the liberal position of the Latin American hierarchy. Within Chile, the evolution of this position has been in process for at least thirty years, but it is only in the last few years that an emphatic change could be observed. The change did not occur without bitter struggles between conservative and liberal priests. For example, in 1958 a conservative priest threatened in a magazine article that any Catholic congressman who voted to relegalize the Communist party risked excommunication. A liberal priest retorted in another magazine that this was an abuse of the idea of excommunication, was not an excommunicable offense, and that a Catholic congressman could vote in conscience for what he believed. Soon after the liberal priest was transferred from the country.

164

Then two men with almost nothing in common made their historic marks, and in so doing alerted the Catholic world. The first was John XXIII, the second, Fidel Castro. Pope John, a mildly socialist man, surveyed Catholic efforts and found them largely irrelevant to the revolution of human aspirations sweeping over the world. He initiated what we now see as "the opening to the left," hoping to embrace those the Church otherwise stood to lose. Castro made the possibility of loss concrete. Systematically he set about to destroy the credibility and effectiveness of the Church in Cuba. Latin America's Catholic priests, shepherds to the largest flock of the faithful in the world, were shaken. Without question, Castro created a receptivity to Pope John's encyclical on social justice, *Mater et Magistra*, that previous encyclicals could not engender.

By 1960 the thinking of Chile's bishops, cumulatively, was about 60 percent traditional, 40 percent liberal. Today 80 percent of the bishops would qualify as liberals on most questions. When the twenty-seven bishops of the Chilean hierarchy assembled in 1964 to set up an integrated plan for the Church throughout the country, they chose eleven from their group to act as the steering committee. All eleven were from the Church's left wing; they had favored the elimination of the traditional cassock and Latin liturgy long before the Council of Rome. Led by the committee, the bishops programmed a vigorous plan in the field of social reform. Remarked one priest, happily: "Planning is coming into the affairs of the Holy Ghost."

Today Chilean bishops stress to employers that in addition to giving to charity they are obliged to pay good wages. The Church is taking a hard look at its school systems, asking whether the schools have tended to create and perpetuate a conservative elite. Extensive contacts with the upper class are also under scrutiny, on the assumption that such contact has tended to alienate the Church from the masses. More concretely, the Church has begun to give away its lands under agrarian reform; it took this step, first, in the hope that its action will inspire others, and second, because, in the words of Father Roger Vekemans, "insofar as the wealth exists, it is a source of embarrassment to the Church."

Already the Church's experience has provided guidelines for the government's agrarian reform program. In a pilot program with two hundred families, Church experts found it essential to put the farmers to work building roads, fences, barns and troughs—before actually farming. When the farmers do receive the land, they will have learned that by pooling resources they can achieve what they never would alone. But the functional importance of the Church's agrarian reform is outweighed by its symbolic significance. "The gesture of the bishops was terribly important," says one well-placed Chilean. "If there had been no example set by the Church, there would have been very little action on the part of the government. Land reform would have been much more violent. And there would have been much more opposition on the part of the vested interests."

Today there is no social problem the Church is unwilling to discuss—a condition that is rather spectacularly demonstrated by the attitude of many Chilean priests toward birth control. They are for it—citing the injunction by several popes, including the present one, that Catholic families have a Christian duty to govern the size of their families by their capacity to provide a good life. But many of Chile's priests favor birth control for other reasons as well. They accept the demographers' conclusion that unless the size of population is controlled, the effects of economic development are dissipated. While the birthrate in

Chile is not so high as in Latin America generally (if present rates are maintained the area's population will triple by the year 2000), it is nonetheless sufficient to retard economic growth and thereby deprive those already on earth of a decent life.

A more urgent cause of the priests' concern is the rate of abortion in Chile. These rates, first announced in 1963 and amplified since, sent shock waves through the hemisphere; studies in almost every Latin American country produced similarly distressing results. In Chile, in 1961 alone, there were 129,000 abortions—one for every two live births. Induced abortions terminated between 35 and 40 percent of all pregnancies. Of 1890 women interviewed at random in a 1962 study made in Santiago, 26 percent had had criminal abortions. A majority had had several. Fifteen women alone accounted for 187 criminal abortions—13 percent of the total. On the basis of these findings, it is estimated there were 25,000 criminal abortions in Santiago in 1962. A survey director, Dr. Tegualda Monreal, declared: "We think it is quite representative. The results could be related to other cities."

There is ample proof that most Latin American families —most of whom call themselves Catholics—want to limit the number of their children, and are willing to violate Church doctrine to do so.

It had always been assumed that lower-class families had more children than upper-class families because they wanted them. Research has now riddled this assumption. J. Mayone Stycos, director of Cornell University's International Population Program and the leading authority on the subject in Latin America, declares:

> If you ask, "Would you rather not have two of your children?" of course, the answer is no. But if you ask, "If you had to do it all over again, how many children would you

have?" they give you a number less than the number they have. Studies of Catholics in Santiago show the lower classes to be overwhelmingly in favor of having small families and . . . generally favorable toward birth control when they know what it is.

Two-fifths of the women queried in one Chilean survey said they were in favor of birth control for families with low incomes; two-fifths favored birth control for those whose health might be endangered, and only one-fifth were unalterably opposed to birth control. Ninety-two percent of the women questioned were Catholic.

Every study of Catholic attitudes toward birth control provide approximately the same conclusion. A paper on Latin America's population problems by Carmen Miró and Jorge Somoza of the Latin American Demographic Center in Santiago might well sum up the case for Chile:

> It is clear that the behavior of Catholics is not the same in the different levels of life and culture. The Catholic couples who live in great cities and enjoy a high level of living that they hope to preserve and better for their children do not act, in reference to birth control, in the same manner as couples residing in rural areas. . . . The doctrinal position of the Catholic Church is not an obstacle to birth control. The persistence of a high birthrate in Latin America cannot be attributed to the predominantly Catholic condition of the population, but to the backward economic and social situation. If the obstacles that impede development were removed . . . the religion of the people would not be an impediment to the reduction of the high birthrate.

Chilean priests now realize that when Chilean Catholics are confronted with the choice of mortal sin or more children, they will choose mortal sin. The reaction of the priests has been unmistakable.

Publicly, the priests carefully point out that birth control should be achieved only by the Church-approved natural method. Privately, however, many of them deplore this method as ineffective, particularly among the uneducated. One Chilean clergyman articulates a common view of the younger, liberal priests: "Our people badly need birth limitation. We should have been working years and years ago to find a solution. Up to now no solution has been found. I deny strongly from the scientific point of view that a real method to check the world's population problem has been found." He sees the rhythm system as presently unworkable for people who cannot read or count, and other contraceptive systems—the moral issue aside—as either too expensive or sophisticated: "The Catholic Church sees the need for control. Why doesn't it talk about it? Because it has no answer. And that's where the Church is guilty. The Church must say clearly that limitation of birth is a duty."

With no effective answer to offer, many priests are loathe to openly resist those who do have an answer. Workers in birth-control programs report that they have not met a single instance of resistance by the Church, even though they are introducing forbidden contraceptive devices. One doctor, the head of a hospital where women who request intrauterine devices are fitted with them, reports indirect word from the Church that it would not formally object: "There's an unwritten agreement. We don't bother them. They don't bother us. If we advertise in the papers, we've got a fight on our hands, but if we rely on word of mouth we've got plenty of work to do."

One young Chilean priest, whose work is mainly among slum dwellers, explains: "It's really difficult to be too strict with them on matters like that when you see how they live." A doctor reports: "To have a child when you want to have a child, when you are in love, that is the most beautiful thing. The young priests understand this. From them we receive an indirect authorization. The priest says to the lady who's had difficulty, 'Go to the physician. Perhaps he can resolve your problem.' You feel the backing to take a wider attitude." A professor at a Catholic hospital, he explains: "I am a physician not only for Catholics. I know as a Catholic I haven't the right to impose my ideas on people who don't think as I think. It would not be correct if I taught only Catholic ideas. I am a scientist. We have a department for instruction in the licit method. The physicians who attend this department are Catholics. And we have a department for illicit methods. This is attended by physicians who are not Catholics." The choice of method, this doctor stressed, is left to the individual: "We wash our hands. It is not our decision. I cannot say, 'You can't do that.' It is a position of you inside. Although we are both Catholics, we have different ideas.

"I know that many in the U.S. will say that this is hypocrisy. We do the best we can with an open mind and heart. I am not in contact with the Church on this problem. You're obliged to make a decision when you have strong responsibility." Like many of his colleagues, this doctor believes that the Church's position on oral contraceptives has not been made clear—or had not, in any event, at the time we spoke. He said: "Where the position is not clear, the Catholic has the right to use his own judgment."

As far as the bishops of Chile were concerned, however, the day seemed not far away when a clear position could be expressed. A strong indication of their thinking appeared in May 1964, in *Mensaje*, a Jesuit magazine published in Santiago. Its editors argued that progestogene synthetic pills, which inhibit ovulation but do not destroy any eggs, are permissible. Progestogene, said the priests, is simply a duplication by man of the natural substance progesterone, which the female body begins to produce once an egg is fertilized in order to prevent further ovulation. This natural protection continues through pregnancy and lactation. The nub of the argument is that such protection can and should be taken over by man after the child is weaned. By limiting family size, man increases the likelihood of a humane setting for the child. Said an editorial preface to the article:

> The child is not only a body, but a human being, which has to be fed, clothed, educated, . . . Nature, in her intrinsic dynamism, tends to assure the future of that child, logically, as far as she can. Will it then be unlawful that man, making use of his intelligence, supplements, assures and continues this direction of nature? Of course not.
>
> Taking off from the base that parents not only have to procreate but make possible the normal human development of their children, the Church accepts the regulation of births. It is what has been called, and rightly so, responsible procreation. Why then not accept the use of the progestogenes that do nothing but substitute for and continue the natural dynamism of nature?

Early in 1964 the bishops of Chile considered drafting a pastoral letter to announce that Catholic women might begin taking progestogene pills. But when Pope Paul VI asked priests to refrain from further independent comment the letter was dropped.

There are two ways in which the reaction to the problem of birth control ought to be pondered. First, it illuminates the modern clerical mind in Chile; the young priest, well-educated, liberally oriented, socially conscious, contrasts strikingly with popular notions of the clergy. Second, the episode demonstrates a feeling for change (both within and without the Church) so strong that it challenges the most sacred of assumptions about the social paralysis. Birth control has always been considered *the* unmentionable, insoluble problem; today its solution is openly, actively pursued. It seems fair to hope, therefore, that whatever the problem in Chilean society, there is no reason why it cannot be attacked—and ultimately solved.

Some pathetically amusing contradictions characterize the effort to limit family size. While the government is giving out contraceptive devices in its hospitals, it is also awarding tax benefits for fecundity. But at this stage of Chilean development the important act is not the accomplished deed, but the idea of change itself.

More than anything Chile needs momentum. What social-action Catholicism can do to provide it has yet to be determined. But already there are strong indications that the effect can be profound.

The matter will not be left to chance. The imperative for change from organized Catholicism is being proffered with system and force. The center of this social-action complex is a brain trust of Chilean Jesuits known as Centro Bellarmino, and the force within the force is the Belgian-born priest Roger Vekemans. Few men in Latin America are more important, controversial or effective.

John F. Kennedy considered him an invaluable commentator on the Latin American reality. George Meany calls him "that Communist priest." Young liberal priests throughout the hemisphere—whom he laughingly refers to as "the Mafia"—look to him for leadership and advice. Conservative priests find him shocking. He has been called "the most powerful priest in Latin America" because of the money he controls as well as the influence he wields in the high councils of the Church. One day in 1965, he arrived late at a meeting in Chicago of the inner group of an international convention of priests involved in Latin American affairs. Immediately, Monsignor Luigi Ligutti of the Vatican, an expert on Latin America and an intimate of the last three popes, crossed the room and embraced him. "The gesture was not lost on the assembled multitude," a priest who was there recalls. Within Chile, he has been the enemy first of the extreme Right, and then of the extreme Left. By 1963 conservatives were calling him a Communist and a subversive, and pressuring his provincial to expel him from Chile. At some point in 1964 the attack switched. The Communist press thought it had found a way, through Vekemans, to attack Frei. Vekemans, the newspaper declared, was clericalizing the Christian Democratic party and politicizing the Church. So persistent were the attacks that Vekeman's provincial arranged for his absence from Chile during the inauguration of Frei, as insurance against any Communist-inspired incident.

Both his person and his manner exude power. Tall and sturdy, his massive head is accentuated by a receding crown of grey hair and small, unwavering eyes that narrow when he is intent or angry, widen and curl when he is pleased. He speaks in imperatives and with certainty. One morning a few years ago, a U.S. industrialist emerged from a wide-ranging breakfast discussion with Vekemans in Santiago and said in awe: "That's one of the most articulate men I've ever met—and he wasn't even speaking his own language."

Vekemans seems omnipresent and indefatigable. At least twenty weeks a year he flies to the United States or Europe on Monday to lobby for funds, returns on Friday for a weekend of work. He accommodates himself with ease to either luxury or poverty. Once, as a guest at the Brussels, a choice New York restaurant, he challenged the captain to make him a *steak tartare* in the Belgian fashion. When the dish came, he tasted it, then, grinning mischievously, blessed the restaurant. But in Santiago, his small, stark room, cluttered with working papers, would not please a pauper.

Questioners frequently ask him how he got to Chile. "That's quite simple," he answers. "I was sent. The mail comes under your door: a letter from the Superior in Rome, a very short letter, telling you, 'Come to Rome.'" In Rome he learned that he had been assigned to Chile. He confesses: "I didn't know where Chile was, so I had to find out."

He had been studying in Paris with Jesuits influenced by Pope Leo XIII, synthesizing almost twenty years of work in philosophy, theology and sociology that had taken him through Europe and provided him with seven languages. He arrived in Chile at the age of thirty-five and reacted violently: "I was shocked, deeply shocked. Latin American Catholicism is plain people's opiate. No osmosis. No symbiosis. I never participated in this kind of spirituality. I'm not Latin; I admit it. I'm Belgian. From Brussels. Clear mind of the French. But German, too, so I don't give up. I push." He realized almost immediately that theory was not going to solve the basic problems of Chile: "I got into the Chilean reality very fast. I came down little by little from the clouds of pure scholarship. If you try to solve it alone you're dead. You've got to deal with technology, with prices, with social security. Reality forced me beyond doctrine, beyond principle, beyond ethics."

In an almost totally disorganized setting, the force of his personality was overwhelming. Here was an organized man. He knew what to do, how to do it and where to get the resources. He saw what others saw, but with fresh eyes; theirs were fogged by time. He was better trained and probably more intelligent. Suddenly, he was the man to see in Chile.

By the intensity of his manner he magnetized those who would never have worked for a lesser man. Yet his sense of urgency was also his greatest liability. People deferred to him and he got used to deference. He did not change his manner, even as the quality of those around him rose. He was sometimes too direct. Once, when a colleague suggested that they organize outings for workers, Vekemans snapped impatiently: "You're dealing with a power structure, and you have to organize on a power basis." He did not appreciate how strongly he affected others. At one point he became cross with a young assistant, said things he didn't mean, then promptly forgot the episode. Now he is puzzled because the young man, whom he genuinely likes, dislikes him. "He doesn't handle himself subtly," a critical admirer observes. "He has a personal arrogance, a lack of humility. He's really not very tolerant of others' views. He says, 'I've made up my mind, and this is it.'" But the critic adds quickly: "He is one of the most intelligent, best-motivated men I know."

More than his person, more than his manner, it was his idea of what was wrong that most caused discomfort. He said that the social structure itself needed to be reorganized. Conservatives pointed out that his father had been a Marxist; the American ambassador said that some of his writings were appeals to class struggle. In a sense they were. What the critics missed was the distinction of method. Vekemans preached a *kind* of class struggle; his battle plan called for the integration of all the forces of the democratic Left, particularly to include those marginal people who had always before been excluded from any social struggle. His diagnosis could not have been more correct. "You are fighting on the wrong front," he told an American. "The Alliance for Progress is between governments. That's not where the fight is going on. It's going on at the bottom." If he did not believe in government, it was because government had failed in the past; if he believed that a social revolution was necessary, it was because he could see that without it conditions would remain the same. He disturbed people because he articulated the needs of the deprived. "My only originality," he once said, "is that I'm living at the bottom with these people—and I can get their words to the top. I've been functioning as a loudspeaker."

To fulfill his battle plan, Vekemans modernized the department of sociology at Catholic University, so that within several years he could have a reserve of well-trained social scientists. At the same time he set up his brain trust, Centro Bellarmino, modeled after the Jesuit center he had attended in Paris. He rented an old mansion on Santiago's main thoroughfare, Alameda Bernardo O'Higgins, and gathered a cosmopolitan staff of twenty Jesuits—Chileans, Belgians, an Argentine, a German and a North American— each highly specialized in at least one discipline, each available to anyone needing expert advice. When the Chilean Church decided to give its lands to agrarian reform, for example, it was able to call upon Gonzalo Arroyo, a tall, thin priest in his mid-thirties with four university degrees, the last a Ph.D. in rural economics from Iowa State.

Like Vekemans, the other Jesuits did not confine themselves to scholarship, but plunged into the Chilean reality of poverty, slums and marginal life. "No cultural-intellectual activity is conceivable unless it's loaded with social emotion," Vekemans declares. "We wanted them to

176

be contaminated day and night by the social emergency. On the other hand, we don't want social action to degenerate into pure activism. We need people with cold insights."

Beginning in the late 1940's, a handful of worker-priests received permission to live in the *callampas* with the poor; their presence did much to reassure those with whom they came in contact that the Church cared about their plight. But the contacts were limited; the priests were few and the poor were many; cynicism prevailed. Destitute rural workers had been drifting to the cities in search of better conditions. There, frequently, trained Communist party workers would help them settle and find work. In 1960 a fight developed between the peasants and the authorities over their right to settle on vacant land at the city's edge. The owner of the land had obtained a restraining order from a court. One dark night, the Argentine Jesuit attached to Bellarmino led thousands of squatters onto the land. The court ordered the priest jailed, but the Church had made an extraordinary point: it was with the people. "That's what we're for—to get in trouble," Vekemans notes. "Whenever news arrives in Rome, some of our men are on it."

For several years Vekemans and his colleagues drew together the facts of the social problem; in 1962 they published their sober, factual and frightening analysis: *Revolution in Latin America*. Their timing was unbelievably opportune; publication came just after the demise of the Church in Cuba. Now the Church knew that it was fighting for its life, and turned to the brain trust for help.

But arousing the Church was only part of Vekemans' battle plan. "We are using priests here only because they are cheaper personnel," he explained. "We have to enter action, not because of clericalism, but because of the need.

177

As soon as there are enough laymen, the priest has to disappear." Vekemans sought to organize non-Church elements through the establishment of an agency with no links to the Church. Known by its Spanish initials, DESAL, the Center for Economic and Social Development of Latin America was at the heart of his plan—the organization of the marginal sectors of society. "What we would like to do," he explained to a reporter once, "is to make a new fabric of society, but always from the bottom up. We want to find channels to bring man closer to the power structure."

For the money to finance DESAL's projects, Vekemans drew on foundations and governments as well as the Church. With his own people, his approach was highly partisan. "Are you a Catholic?" he demanded of Germany's Joseph Cardinal Frings one day.

Startled, the Cardinal laughed. "What do you mean?" he said.

"Are you a good Catholic who loves his neighbor, his brother Catholic?"

"Of course," the Cardinal said.

"Who are your brother Catholics?" Vekemans challenged. "One-third of them are in Latin America. Did you know that?"

"Yes," the Cardinal said.

"Why, if you know that, do you give only 7 percent of your money to Latin America—and half of that to Germans in Latin America?"

Again the Cardinal laughed. "Okay," he said, "From now on, at least one-third of our money goes to Latin America."

Once there, however, the money immediately loses identity. It ceases to be "Church" money, and becomes, instead, Latin American money, handled by Latin Americans.

178

Today the millions of dollars raised by Vekemans and his DESAL colleagues finance six hundred projects in every Latin American country save Cuba and Brazil, all of them under the auspices of the development agency in Santiago, all of them related to some form of community development for marginal people—neighborhood associations, workshops, radio schools, savings and loan associations, co-ops, and trade unions. DESAL is even involved in family planning. Whatever the organization does, its operation is strictly business. Charity, it has learned, breeds resentment, destroys the moral fibre of man. "Nothing is donated," Vekemans says. "There is no charity at all. In our idea, charity is worse than communism. All our money is basically loans. We never give anything away."

In less than a decade Vekemans has accomplished more than most men do in a lifetime. Inevitably, he has made mistakes. At one time or another he has managed to offend elements of his Church, the Christian Democratic party, and the U.S. labor movement, which is deeply involved in social reform in Latin America. But given the conditions that he encountered at the outset, it is doubtful that he could have done what he did with less abrasive tactics. Not even his critics could fail to concede his two major contributions to Chilean momentum. The first: he helped solidify the *idea* that change is possible. The second: he dramatized the dynamics of social-action Catholicism.

It would be too much to say that change in Chile pivots on the insinuation of Catholic social doctrine into human affairs. But it would be no exaggeration to say that the occurrence not only represents a striking change in its own right, but a substantial factor favoring change as well. Added to the political dynamics of Christian Democracy, it makes a potent brew.

Church and state remain carefully separated in Chile

and no one in power on either side would have it any other
way. Each takes its separate path. But Chile is a small
country and a Catholic one; ultimately, there is a point at
which the paths of modern Catholicism and Christian
Democracy converge. That point is found in man himself.

> Today in Chile, [the Reverend Mark McGrath wrote a
> few years ago] the most gifted youth of the country, in terms
> of intelligence, culture and social position, belong to the great
> families of the past, among whom, along with their immediate
> circle of workers and employees, one can find a large propor-
> tion of those 10 to 15 percent of Chilean Catholics who
> assist at mass every Sunday. The social preeminence they en-
> joy signifies privilege and responsibility. By and large, they
> and their parents have enjoyed the privileges and overlooked
> the responsibility. But now there is *inquietud*. Translated into
> reality, *inquietud* means a sense of the emptiness of the social
> round of parties and long summers at the beach and high
> living to no purpose. "Spiritual formation" is in serious de-
> mand.

McGrath might have been summarizing the story of my
friend Guillermo Videla Vial, who embodies for me all the
changes that could transform Chile one day.

The Videla Vial family is one of the oldest in Chile; it lists
a former president of the country and a member of the Senate; it is devoutly Catholic and traditionally conservative
—a model, in short, of the Chilean Establishment. Out-
wardly Guillermo would seem an exemplar of his class. In
his early thirties, he is tall, slim, strikingly handsome,
suffused with Latin graces, a golfing stylist. To his class,
however, he is a traitor. "They are very disappointed in
me," he joked one day. "I am very disappointed in them."

An only child, he grew up a virtual prince. His father
was the resident manager of a French-owned coal mining
company in southern Chile, whose shafts reach under the

bed of the Pacific Ocean for several miles. The family lived in a big home provided by the company, set on a cliff overlooking the ocean, surrounded by acres of formal gardens maintained by workers from the rows of drab company houses nearby. Except for Sundays, when the miners and their families were permitted to enter, the garden was Guillermo's alone.

Through his first years in college, Guillermo lived in an insulated, upper-class Catholic environment. Then he matriculated at the University of Chile to study law. There, for the first time, he met Chileans from different backgrounds. "Their arguments were different," he recalls. "Before, this game was better than that game, this girl was better than that girl. Now, suddenly, these people were arguing ideas, and challenging the validity of your very life."

Guillermo completed his studies and began to practice law. But he was restless and unhappy. The criticism of his classmates haunted him, particularly that of the Communists. But he had no ideology to counter theirs. Spiritually, he was Catholic, but he was appalled by what the Church had come to represent. And what the Chilean Establishment had produced, he did not accept. He could see that it provided no life for the great mass of Chileans. "I won't go to the street to defend the democracy we have now," he told me in 1961.

Then, one day, Guillermo found a new client, and life was never the same again. The client was an organization called *Techo*, which in Spanish means roof. Started by priests, but neither confessional nor political, *Techo* was an economic and social response to the problems of slum dwellers. Its aim was to incorporate marginal workers into the productive life of the country by giving them access to the means of production. *Techo* would translate slum dwellers from beggars into workers, ultimately into owners. The economic result would be secondary, the psychological result, primary.

One *Techo* project dealt with scavengers who lived with their families alongside the Santiago garbage dump. Each day these men would haul crude rented carts through the city, picking up discarded clothing, rags, boxes. At the dump they would receive two cents a kilo for the rubbish. Half of the proceeds would be paid in bread and wine. The other half would be retained as rent by the owner of the carts—who would then resell the rubbish for twenty-five cents a kilo.

Techo encouraged the scavengers to scrape enough materials together to build several carts of their own. Before long, they were not only rid of the middleman, they had collected enough money to open a bank account—whose symbolic worth was infinitely more valuable than the small deposit. Soon they had saved enough money to buy an old truck. Finally, they built a sorting plant, which meant a much higher price for the refuse.

Many families now live from this labor. But the important fact is that the men involved, who never thought that they were capable of accomplishing anything, now believed that they were.

"Poor people don't want things, they want possibilities," Guillermo said to me on top of the garbage dump one day in 1962. "The principal necessity is not bread, clothes and a roof. The principal necessity is culture. The Communist party doesn't give things. It gives ideas, possibilities. The Communist party has never given gifts to those people. The solution of giving is an aspirin. It gets at the symptom, but it doesn't cure. The public already has a lot of morphine. It

wants a remedy. Charity makes beggars of the poor. Getting
accustomed to being given everything instead of fighting for
it, they put out their hands. All sense of fight they should
have is lost. If when they are hungry we give them beans,
if when they need a house we give them a house, they will
continue being hungry and being members of a slum. We
must give them a possibility. The most important thing in
life is to feel useful. Think of the problem these people
have—they never feel useful for anything."

We passed a little boy. "Look at this child," he said.
"Look at that face. Intelligent, no? Yet he is doomed to a
life of a dollar a day." We came upon a scavenger Guillermo knew, an old man with deep lines and a sunburned
face, who was picking rubbish apart atop the garbage pile.
Guillermo embraced the man warmly, and they spoke for
several minutes. Afterward, he said: "If you go inside that
man, you will see how rich he is in human condition. He is
ready to be occupied. If we don't do it, someone else will. I
know that we are twenty years late—Marxism gave an answer first. I hope we won't be late again. That depends on
me, people who have everything like me. If we come late,
it's going to be our fault. No Chilean with a good home can
go to bed at night with his conscience clear if he is not
doing something to help the slums."

He took me into a church the slum dwellers had built.
There were holes in the roof and the siding. The windows
had no glass. Guillermo looked at me with satisfaction.
"This is the way all the churches of Santiago should be—
no better than the homes of the people who come to it."

Outside, we talked about the Church. "Why didn't this
happen twenty years ago? The fault was the Church. I
know that in the last two hundred years the rich people
have used the Church as a means of exploitation. They

have had the Church say, 'You are poor here, but you will be rich in Heaven.' But the Catholic Church is not the priests or the pope. Who are the Church? We. We formed the Church, the Mystical Body of Christ. I beg you to understand that I am the Church. We all are the Church. The priests have a position in the Church, but they are not the Church."

For the Church, Guillermo is the fruit of its own change. "I would not have worked for the old Church," he says. But a Church that can produce *Techo* is another matter. "It's a Christian movement, but not with a big sign. Our best propaganda with these people is not to have propaganda."

When Guillermo started, the priests suggested that he work among his own class. He didn't want to. "The problem is so urgent we can't waste time trying to make people understand who have so much difficulty understanding," he said. When he tried to explain and obtain support for his work, the Establishment would respond that the Church had no business getting involved in such things. Their response delighted Guillermo. "When the people of the high part of the city go against the Church, that means the Church is on the right track with the people. I am going to be very happy when a man comes to confession and the priest asks, 'Where do you work?' and the man says, 'I am the manager of a bank,' and the priest asks, 'How much do you pay your workers?' and the man answers, 'So much,' and the priest says, 'Well, I won't give you absolution until you pay more.'

"We must destroy many things. We must suffer a lot. Many people must go against us. We are bulldozers. We must do this work now, the bulldozer work. After, will come the engineer to build the road. I am sure that I won't ever see the road, but we must clear the path."

184

Perhaps he was overcautious. Today, *Techo* is working with 50,000 Chileans. Even more significantly, it serves as a model and inspiration—particularly in terms of its psychological insights—for the government's *Promoción Popular*. And Guillermo himself has made great strides. In 1963 he left *Techo* to work for Eduardo Frei. Today he is General Director of Labor, and the government's chief troubleshooter in the field. His transitional life makes him a natural bridge between extreme Left and Right.

Roger Vekemans once said that change in Chile was "basically a generation problem." Guillermo Videla is a product of many forces that simply did not exist twenty years ago. In his work and thought he embodies the deep change in Chile today.

9

The United States and Chile

It was one of those miraculous Chilean days—clear, warm, balmy, with just enough wind to carry the fragrance of orange blossoms and fuchsias—so much like a bygone California at its best. The four Chileans and three Americans had finished a leisurely luncheon at the home of Robert Stevenson in the Barrio Alto, a half hour from the center of Santiago. Now, before returning to their offices downtown, they adjourned to the garden to have coffee and complete their conversation. Their discussion was about labor and they spoke in Spanish. In addition to Stevenson, political counselor of the U.S. embassy, the Americans were Tom Walsh, the labor attaché, and Rudy Fimbres, second secretary at the embassy. The Chileans were Willie Thayer, a leading Christian Democrat (later to be secretary of labor in the Frei cabinet), José de Gregorio, secretary general of the CD party, Rafael Agustín, a CD deputy to Congress, and Serafino Romualdi, Inter-

American representative of the AFL-CIO. It was 2:30 P.M., November 22, 1963.

Shortly thereafter, Stevenson excused himself to answer the phone. He returned moments later, distressed. "The embassy just called," he said. "There's been an assassination attempt on President Kennedy."

The men gazed at one another in silence and apprehension. With difficulty, they resumed their discussion. But a few minutes later, when the phone rang again, their voices faded.

Stevenson walked swiftly into the house. When he returned, his face was white. "The President's been shot," he said. "He's been taken to the hospital."

Now all the guests rose. They agreed that it was best for them to return at once to their offices. But before they could say good-bye, the telephone rang for the third time. Stevenson ran to answer. In a moment, he returned. His eyes brimmed with tears. He said, "The President is dead."

The men looked incredulously at one another. Then the Chileans turned to the Americans, opened their arms, and embraced them in turn. That done, each of the men found a place in the garden alone. Finally, they turned again, embraced once more, and went their separate ways.

Downtown, the newspapers carried the headlines of the assassination attempt. But everyone had heard the radio bulletins and knew that Kennedy was dead. Pedestrians walked aimlessly, stunned, bewildered. Crowds clustered at shop windows to watch television sets. In one crowd, a woman sobbed openly. "Why are you crying?" her four-year-old son kept asking.

Twenty minutes after confirmation of Kennedy's death, Jorge Alessandri Rodríguez, the Chilean president, accompanied by his military aide, several ministers and the chief

187

of protocol, walked across the square from *La Moneda* to the American embassy to express condolences to the U.S. ambassador, Charles W. Cole. Then Alessandri returned to the presidential palace and declared three days of national mourning. Kennedy's "tragic death is not only sorrowful for sister countries of the United States of America," the Chilean president stated. "It is the entire world which in these hours feels the anguish of an irreparable loss. All of Chile joins in this sorrow, because in him it found deep understanding of its problems and a will always determined to help us."

All through Chile, at every level, the reaction to Kennedy's death was overwhelming. "It was worse than if you had told me that Alessandri had died," a leading politician said bluntly. "More Chileans were identified with Kennedy than with Alessandri. Kennedy signified the possibility of a transformation. Alessandri didn't signify anything." The reaction was as intense on the Left as on the Right. A leftist friend of Rudy Fimbres', who believed (as did most leftists), that Kennedy had been the victim of a political plot, told him: "I will never forgive you for what you did to your President." To a man, the Christian Democrats were stunned. They had fashioned themselves the New Frontiersmen of Chile; their identification with Kennedy had been profound. They felt now as though they had lost a leader of their own.

Moments after Alessandri's departure from the U.S. embassy, crowds of visitors began to arrive; they included congressmen, clergymen, political leaders, government officials, union men and friends of the United States. Special editions of afternoon tabloids carried nothing but news of the assassination. Radio stations cancelled all commercials, programmed classical music until after the funeral

1 8 8

the following Monday. The next morning, Santiago newspapers appeared with black mourning borders. Even the Communist newspaper, *El Siglo*, abandoned the red type that always distinguished its masthead. For three days all political campaigning halted. And on Monday, as Richard Cardinal Cushing offered a pontifical requiem mass for the murdered President, Raúl Cardinal Silva Henríquez did the same in Santiago. Before the altar rested a symbolic coffin, draped with an American flag. In kneeling chairs near the coffin, President Alessandri, his ministers and armed forces chiefs mourned. Behind them, praying Chileans, jammed together, knelt in the pews and aisles. Outside, thousands more, unable to get into the church, knelt in the streets.

The extraordinary reaction to the death of Kennedy illuminated, as perhaps nothing else could, the complex depths of feeling Chileans have for the United States. Most Americans assume it is nothing but a compound of animosity, hostility and contempt. Kennedy's death revealed an emotion as delicate and contradictory as that of a boy for an older brother. Kennedy did not know Chile, but his words indicated that he understood the psychological components of underdevelopment—the craving for change, the sense of frustration and inferiority, the outraged pride. To protect himself, a smaller brother must assume a belligerent pose; a death in the family unmasks his love.

Ours is a big brother's legacy. Involuntarily we impose our way of doing things on smaller countries. Our styles mold theirs; our moods set modes. But as we entice, we also threaten. A smaller brother feels overwhelmed, engorged. He yearns for our effectiveness. But he wants to be himself.

International politics is hard to grasp. Its concerns

189

seem too vast and remote. Yet decisions are ultimately made by ordinary beings who harbor the conventional set of human emotions. A Latin American may love more intensely, hate more selectively, or anger more immediately, but he reacts within a human arena. In many ways, the relations between nations are as intensely human as that of one being for another.

For almost a decade now, we Americans have been casting about in bewilderment for clues to what is "wrong" with our policy in Latin America. We have made studies, designed programs and fashioned pacts. We have offered assistance, sent people and spent money. Our efforts have produced progress. But just as we think we are getting somewhere, something happens—a Bay of Pigs, a Dominican crisis—and from the outcries, one could only conclude that, once again, we were brandishing the Big Stick.

Our technical approach to the problems of Latin America is excellent. It should not be forsaken because of momentary setbacks. A European diplomat serving in Latin America once said something very wise to Pat Holt, the U.S. Senate Foreign Relations Committee staff consultant: "There is nothing worse than abandoning a good long-range policy because of short-range difficulties." Perhaps it is time, therefore, to look beyond technology to the human factors of our policy.

We do not treat Latin America like a brother. We treat it like a child. We are paternal and distrustful. In the past, Latin America has often deserved our treatment; it has been churlish, undisciplined, irresponsible. But if we *must* act like parents, we ought to be sensitive ones. We should watch closely for signs that our child is becoming a man.

It is a delicate matter indeed to distinguish rebellion from maturation. Often the only way to tell is to take a

190

chance. We are very much in the predicament of the father who has finally given his young son the car for the evening. He lies awake, straining for the sound of wheels crunching gravel, wondering if he will ever see his child alive again. It would have been so much easier and more comfortable not to have given the car. But the boy must become a man; the parent must let him go.

In the technical field, we have talked man to man. In the human field, we have failed to let go. In the subtlest of ways, we emasculate our ward.

Much of Latin America's fear of domination may be fanciful and self-induced. But much is historically accurate. The ringing proclamation of James Monroe sounded marvelous to North American ears, but it produced an entirely different response in Diego Portales.

With the U.S. intervention in the Dominican Republic modern North Americans, frequently baffled by Latin American charges of Yankee imperialism, could freshen their historical perspective. Newspapers reminded them of three overt precedents—the Mexican War, in which the U.S. gained half of that country's territory by force; the Panama incident, in which the U.S. finessed territory for its canal by encouraging the independence of Panama, then recognized her territorial "claims" against Colombia (the U.S. later paid Colombia $25 million in guilty-conscience money); and the occupation of the banana republics where U.S. Marines "protected" U.S. private investments for sixteen years. Other less spectacular examples of U.S. intervention may be long forgotten by North Americans, but they are Biblical verse to the Chileans.

Few North Americans have ever heard of Lieutenant Carlos Peña, but few educated Chileans would fail to identify him as the martyr of the Baltimore Affair. One evening in October 1899, a group of sailors from the U.S.S. *Baltimore*, which was anchored offshore, went prowling in the red-light district of Chile's major port city, Valparaíso. Relations between the U.S. and Chile were strained; some touchy commercial negotiations were not going well; local newspapers were full of disruptive statements. That night a Chilean sailor and two American sailors argued; the Americans threw rocks, knocking the Chilean down, and the battle was on. One American was killed; another died later of injuries.

The *Baltimore*'s skipper filed a report exonerating his men; the U.S. Government then protested to the government of Chile. Within months, the incident had actually become a threat to the peace. The U.S. let it be known that it was ready to seize Chilean nitrate deposits unless the Chileans apologized. Diplomatic attempts at negotiation were models of bluster and misrepresentation. Finally, Chile agreed to pay $75,000 to the dead sailors' families.

Enter Lieutenant Peña. In addition to the payment, as almost any Chilean will tell you, the agreement required Chile to send a warship to San Francisco (or Valparaíso, depending on who tells the story), there to strike its colors in an act of contrition. It was Lieutenant Peña who lowered the Chilean flag until it brushed the deck, ordered the ship's band to play the Chilean Anthem, and who, flag to his breast, pulled a pistol and put a bullet through his heart.

Lieutenant Peña is sheer invention, as Professor Fredrick Pike documents in his study, *Chile and the United States*, 1880–1962. But he is the only part of the Baltimore Affair that is. Chilean feelings toward the U.S. may be distorted by error, but the errors are interlaced with facts.

Professor Pike indicts the U.S. for attempting to shape

192

the Southern Hemisphere to its liking. Its use of power in behalf of U.S. citizens at the end of the nineteenth century was often brutal—even though their demands were frequently without merit. Incidents with Chile were particularly odious. One U.S. firm, which called itself the North and South American Construction Company, contracted to build railroads in Chile, but never did. Yet, because of U.S. State Department pressure, the Chileans were compelled to make a "settlement" with the company. Commercial and diplomatic functions frequently became obscured. If two countries were disputing a land claim, as did Chile and Peru in the late 1800's, the U.S. would invariably side with the country whose victory would best serve U.S. investors —in this case, Peru. Worse, there were indications that U.S. officials had financial interests in the proceedings.

Some of the conduct of the United States during this period can be explained by its desire to outdo Britain in a battle for markets. Whatever the motivation, however, there is historical evidence to support the Chilean's belief that the North American looked upon Latin America as an area to exploit. The North American might maintain that he was saving weak Peru from strong Chile. The Chileans would maintain that he was saving Peru for himself.

Modern Chileans on both Right and Left, believe that the United States wants to maintain Latin America in a state of underdevelopment, so that the area will remain a market for finished U.S. goods, rather than become a producer in its own right. Most Latin Americans share this opinion. For proof, they cite U.S. favoritism toward other areas of the world. Up to the end of 1963, Latin America had received only $6.2 billion in assistance from the United States. By contrast, Western Europe had received $33 billion—more than three times as much per person.

Alliance for Progress funds have since reduced this ratio, but have not appreciably reduced the impression.

The average non-Marxist Latin American, a poor theorist and vague student, casually accepts a good many Marxist notions about capitalism without really comprehending their origin. He believes, for example, that capitalism must either constantly conquer new foreign markets or perish. He views foreign investment in his country as evil, without knowing that every industrialized country, without exception, experienced a period in which foreign investment served as a catalyst to growth. He succumbs easily to the assertion that U.S. industry "sucks the blood" from his country's veins by remitting huge profits to stockholders abroad. When Adlai E. Stevenson and William Benton toured Chile in 1960, they were assured by numbers of Chileans that the U.S. mining companies—which comprise the bulk of the $1 billion U.S. private investment in Chile—were siphoning off much of Chile's wealth. Investigating, the two Americans found that it simply wasn't so. Wrote Benton later:

> Top-ranking Chilean officials told us that approximately 60 percent of the gross earnings of the U.S. mining companies in Chile goes to the Chilean government in taxes, adding more than $100 million annually to the Chilean budget. That is, of course, over and above the salaries and wages, transportation costs and other payments that go back into the Chilean economy.

Of the remaining 40 percent, the biggest portion pays for operating costs. Much of what then remains is reinvested. Finally a dividend is paid to investors.

But Chileans—and other Latin Americans—scoff at such figures. They assume that the books are crooked; after all, don't their capitalists keep two sets? They believe that U.S.

194

firms import amortized equipment on falsified invoices, which make their investment much lower and their profit, therefore, much higher than they report. They are convinced that through some alchemy—possibly a bribe to fiscal authorities—the Americans are able to take out far more money than they announce.

The burden of their confusion pivots on that dangerous moment in human affairs when people give different meanings to the same words. For example, the North American considers profit a reward for risk. The average Latin American considers profit an indication that he's being exploited. He constantly confuses profit with capital. On countless occasions, I have posed this problem to Latin Americans: "Suppose I invest $10,000 in a business in your country, and make $1000 each year, and each year send my profit home. At the end of ten years, how much would I have invested in your country?" Any North American would quickly respond, "Ten thousand dollars." But the Latin American would answer more often than not, "Nothing. You brought $10,000. You took $10,000 away."

"But what about my investment?" I would ask.

"That belongs here. If you want to use it here, you are welcome. But you may not send more away."

It is weird economics to suggest that an investment base shrinks if profits are paid. Yet that, in effect is the thinking many Latin Americans apply to foreign investments in their country. From their viewpoint, the reasoning is sound. To them, anything a foreigner removes above his investment means a net capital loss to the country.

Such reasoning has made foreign ownership, particularly U.S. ownership, an emotional political issue in Latin America. It was for this reason that President Frei's proposal to form a partnership with American companies—to

Chileanize the copper industry, in effect—had such political merit. By all business standards as well, the program offered an exceptional opportunity for Chile. But for fifteen months a FRAP-Radical-Establishment alliance in the Senate blocked authorization to purchase the shares that formalized the partnership. Given the suspicions of the Chileans, it was not surprising.

In one way or another, for one reason or another, some valid, others not, the average Chilean suspects almost any move involving the Americans. Intervention (which is another term for human domination) is the key that decodes the strained, ambivalent language between the neighbors. It is not so much a matter of being against us as it is of being for themselves—or others like themselves. This feeling is clearly evident in Chilean reaction to the three major episodes of U.S. conflict in Latin America in this decade.

In the 1961 Bay of Pigs invasion, Chilean sentiment was clearly against the United States and with the Cubans. Whatever their judgment of the Castro regime, most Chileans were shocked by the U.S.-financed invasion attempt of Cuban exiles. Only 15.6 percent of a national sample polled by Professor Eduardo Hamuy thought the U.S. support of the Cuban invasion had been a good idea; 61.8 percent were against it. (The others polled had no opinion.) Yet that same year, when Hamuy asked Chileans to evaluate the Cuban Revolution, only 4.5 percent classified it as very good; 25.1 percent thought it was good; 15 percent said it was fair; 39.6 percent thought it was bad; and 5.5 percent considered it very bad. (A few years later, the overwhelming majority of Chileans queried by Hamuy in the wake of Chile's break with Cuba favored maintaining either diplomatic or commercial relations with Cuba. They might disapprove of the Cuban regime, but they do not question its right to exist.)

In the 1962 missile crisis most Chileans, simply as a matter of survival, were opposed to the Cuban-Russian maneuver. Nonetheless they did not believe the U.S. should have intervened unilaterally. Christian Democrats protested in the Chamber of Deputies that the U.S. had taken action without first presenting its evidence to the Organization of American States. The party later deplored the polarization of the world into two power blocs threatening one another's destruction, insisted that encirclement drove the Cubans deeper into the Soviet sphere and denounced the quarantine as going beyond international norms. But the Christian Democrats also scored the USSR for introducing offensive bases in Cuba. The action, they said, was a clear violation of hemispheric security, and the OAS was legitimately entitled to intervene in Cuba in order to verify the presence of the missiles and remove them.

In the 1965 Dominican Republic episode, Chilean reaction was one of intense disgust. Most Chileans viewed the invasion as simply the latest example of the unwillingness of the U.S. to permit any change in the status quo. Their reaction to the landings came slowly, in all probability because they could hardly believe what was happening; it was not long, however, before cordons of Chilean youths had gathered in front of the U.S. chancery, shouting "Down with imperialism." Communist and radical leftists made up only part of the crowd. Many members of the National Council of Christian Democratic Youth were also present. Communist and Socialist dailies headlined alleged U.S. massacres of Dominican people. The papers featured one story from *Prensa Latina*, the Cuban news service, asserting that the U.S. was using tear gas on the people, just as it had begun to do in Vietnam.

The radical Left was more vociferous, but hardly more critical, than the majority of Chileans. When the foreign minister, Gabriel Valdés, issued a governmental request for "immediate and collective action in place of unilateral intervention," his view received wide support from the people. In a public opinion poll only 6.8 percent said they favored the U.S. intervention; 48.8 percent were against it. Because it is characteristic of Chileans to decline to answer rather than answer in the negative, the high proportion of those declining to give an opinion indicates that the number of those opposed to the U.S. action was much higher. Even the conservative, normally pro-U.S. daily, *El Mercurio*, ended an editorial on a critical note.

At the height of the crisis, U.S. ambassador Ralph A. Dungan, accompanied by Foreign Minister Valdés, and Radomiro Tomić, who had been appointed ambassador to the United States, drove south from Santiago to a chicken farm where Frei was sequestered, preparing his State of the Union message. "This is a terrible thing," he told Dungan. "You may gain an island, but you'll lose a continent." The three Chileans admitted that they knew nothing of the actual circumstances in the Dominican Republic. But, they complained, they were boxed in; the U.S. action had given them no room to maneuver among their own people. "This is a Chilean matter; it is not solely of the Christian Democratic party," Frei explained. "It would be political suicide not to go against this." The president had polled the foreign ministers of the last several administrations. To a man they had been critical of the U.S. move.

A few days later, Frei went before Congress and expressed the "solidarity of the people of Chile for the people of the Dominican Republic in their fight for freedom," and called for withdrawal of U.S. troops. Congress applauded mightily.

To Frei the Dominican crisis epitomized the contradiction in U.S. policy toward Latin America. It is, he says, disoriented:

> I believe the United States had not defined with clarity whether it's going to follow the road of a political solution, of political understanding with Latin America, or whether it's going to concentrate its action on a policy of police defense of the established order in these countries. The case of Santo Domingo is an example that illustrates my point. The United States, alarmed by the possibility of a government in which there might exist some Communist influence, decided upon a unilateral act without any previous consultation—an armed intervention. This is a *politic* of emergency for emergency. . . .
>
> The case of Santo Domingo is the culmination of a specific situation. For more than twenty years a dictatorship with the worst possible characteristics existed there. This left the country morally and humanly destroyed. In such a case, it's not easy to get back into a democratic situation. So groups were able to predominate that maintained many of the vices of the old dictatorship, and kept the people completely at the margin of life in their own country.

Months after the invasion, Frei still believed that the U.S. action had snuffed out a legitimate uprising of the Dominican people against a military junta that had illegally evicted a constitutional government. "The U.S. intervention," he told me, "has created a great opposition in public opinion in Latin America. As a consequence, the United States has worsened its position without resolving the fundamental problem in Santo Domingo."

"A lot depends on how things turn out in the Dominican Republic," a U.S. official observed. "If the government is aggressive on economic and social reforms, if we work with the reform elements, okay. But if the Dominican Republic doesn't modify its stand, they (the Chileans) will never forgive us, and we'll never be able to prove that if things hadn't run their course it wouldn't have come out better."

Anyone who wants to know what is wrong with our present policy in Latin America might well start here. There is a link between the Dominican Republic and Chile, between the precipitous decision to intervene and the crisis of confidence that afflicts our efforts throughout the hemisphere.

These are gambling times in Latin America. Does one strike swiftly, determined that there shall not be another Cuba? Or does one wait, hoping first that the new waves of genuine reformers will roll over the Marxist radicals who inevitably accompany any political uprising, and second, that Latin American centrists and liberals will give support? It is not inconceivable that Chile, like other republics that ultimately opposed the U.S. action, might actually have offered assistance to quell the fighting, had U.S. diplomacy been a bit more patient. No one argued the need to restore order and save lives. The U.S. did make a brief attempt at consultation with the Organization of American States, but events quickly overran diplomacy. "The OAS and UN charters and the Rio treaty were all drafted to take care of aggression on nineteenth-century terms," one of the principals to the U.S. decision told me at the height of the crisis. "They did not deal with subversion. Look at Cuba. There were only twelve people in the beginning, and yet they took it over."

Thus action made sense from one point of view. It was a guarantee against another Cuba. But hemispheric support is our vital interest too, for reasons of security, world diplomacy, trade. In reviewing the Dominican crisis with Frei, I posed a hypothetical question to the president, as a means of sharpening my understanding of his thought. The question was this: "If Chile knew tomorrow that Peru was captured by Communist guerrillas, what would be Chile's response?" Frei's answer says a great deal about the sacredness that Latin Americans attach to the principle of self-determination. "If the Peruvian government, legally and democratically constituted, and authentically representative of the Peruvian people, would solicit aid from us, we would be in a situation to consider it. But only on the basis, I repeat, of a decision of the proper government of Peru. Never would we be able to accept an intervention, our intervention, without this categorical condition."

Political domination is human domination—nothing less. Political units react to political domination in a precisely human way. The irony is that our diplomats know this so well. Their theory is splendid. "I don't believe you can expect U.S. economic, social and political systems to be adopted by cultures which are very unlike our own," former Assistant Secretary of State for Economic Affairs, Thomas C. Mann, once said. "Nobody is trying for uniformity, trying to get everybody to do everything exactly alike. But I think we can find a common thread of liberty, economic freedom, political freedom—the basic things— regardless of the forms they take in various countries." Most U.S. diplomats would agree. The problem is that in a moment of doubt or crisis, they instinctively "play it safe." That leads them straight to the current Establishment.

But in Latin America, force is fickle. Our diplomats' strategy may work for a while, but it won't work for long. The forces for change are too persistent.

The hearts of our veterans in Latin American diplomacy are big and generous. But their heads are often full of bitter memories of weak men and broken promises. In the Dominican crisis, the head ruled the heart. History may say that this was right. But we are wooing Latin America, and while the strategy of courtship comes from the head, love, finally, is an affair of the heart.

It is neither inaccurate nor unrealistic to speak of love

between the Americas. Regardless of their outbursts, Latin Americans have an affinity and admiration for North Americans. In Chile, a year before the election of 1964, the Christian Democrats ordered a public opinion survey to determine the effects of a campaign linked in any way to the United States. Many within the party had feared that such a campaign would be disastrous. The results showed that their fears were without foundation. They corroborated inquiries made by Professor Hamuy. Each year since 1957 he has asked Chileans to name the country for which they have the most "sympathy." At the outset, 36 percent named the United States—more by far than any other country. For the next three years, the figure remained the same. In 1961 "sympathy" for the U.S. rose to 40 percent; in 1964 it hit a peak of 49 percent. The Soviet Union, by contrast, hit a peak of 8.4 percent in 1961, four years after the launching of Sputnik. By August 1964 its popularity had fallen to 5 percent. In conjunction, the same sample had been asked each year to name the country for which it felt the least "sympathy." Each year, 10 percent named the U.S.; in 1957, 43 percent indicated the Soviet Union; by 1964 the figure had risen to 50 percent.

What factors have contributed most to "sympathy" toward the U.S.? Surely, one answer is the manner in which President Kennedy made thousands of Latin Americans feel "inarticulately and undemonstrably," as George C. Lodge puts it, that "for the first time . . . their rich and powerful neighbor to the north was genuinely committed to the struggle for social justice; that there was in truth a real alternative to the cynical demagogues of the Left who promised progress but at the cost of becoming their captives; an alternative, also, to the crumbling and decrepit structures of present power."

202

Writing in the January 1966 issue of *Foreign Affairs*, Lodge, director of the division of international activities of the Harvard Graduate School of Business Administration, declared:

> We have a tendency to suppose that actions speak louder than words; yet perhaps the words of President Kennedy were most important in those first years of the Alliance—his assertion that the United States was a revolutionary country, that we profoundly supported the demands of the people of Latin America for radical social, political and economic change, that we were concerned only that the revolution be constructive, serving its own highest and noblest ends, and that its independence be protected against those who would subvert it for imperialistic purposes. These were the words which throughout the hemisphere helped put Mr. Kennedy's picture in the huts of the interior, in workers' housing projects of the cities, in *tiendas* (shops), gas stations and schoolhouses.

A second factor in contributing to sympathy for the U.S. has been U.S. assistance itself. By far the greatest impact the U.S. has ever produced in Chile was in the help it offered the country following the earthquakes of 1960. Figures on the damage to life at the time are in dispute. The Chilean figure is in the neighborhood of 3000 killed; some U.S. scholars maintain that the number has been overly exaggerated. But there is no disputing that thousands were injured and left homeless, that hospitals, schools, roads and bridges were destroyed. United States assistance was immediate, generous and decisive. "You sent people, not just supplies," the Chileans repeated to the Americans. They especially admired the lack of drum-beating. A newspaperman who sometimes criticized the U.S. marveled that a field hospital bore no sign advertising 'U.S. Army.' Chileans were amazed to see Negro and white medical troops, officers and enlisted men, working side by side. Taxi drivers, storekeepers, and shoe-shine boys refused to let the soldiers pay for anything. At one 2 A.M. departure from Chile, kitchen men in the local hotel insisted on getting up to cook breakfast for the men housed there. The hotel refused to accept payment. At the airport 5000 Chileans saw them off.

United States assistance to Chile, which began on a small scale in 1945, has been estimated at almost $1 billion today. In addition to reconstruction after the earthquakes, the money has been used for rural electrification, port and highway construction, a jet airport and railroads, mining and agricultural improvements, public health projects and savings and loan associations. The money has also enabled the Chileans to acquire important industrial machinery, provided training for engineers and scholarships for university students to study in the United States. The Food for Peace Program is also funded through U.S. aid, as is the U.S. portion of the cost of the Chile-California Program, one of whose products was the penetrating analysis of educational deficiencies made by several California professors.

Only a small portion of these funds is given in the form of outright grants. The remainder are loans to be paid back over a long period. The rates of these loans are concessionary—that is, the interest is so low that it cannot be considered "good business." It is not meant to be. The object is to provide over an interim period external resources that the economy is incapable of producing itself. The government will have a financial breathing spell until 1971; hopefully, it will be able to create a society capable of financing expansion and able to pay back loans at normal rates.

Without the Alliance, Frei would have to impose a much

starker regime on his people. With the Alliance, he can not only ease the pain of change, he can generate assistance that would not otherwise flow. In certain instances, money the Chileans use to "pay" for machinery and Food for Peace products is then loaned back for the building of schools, hospitals, and other projects.

United States officials are virtually unanimous in their praise of the Frei administration's efforts to achieve reforms in harmony with development—a process that goes to the heart of the Alliance. "The new Chilean government is a beautiful example of what you need to make the Alliance work," says one U.S. participant. "You have to have a government willing to disturb internal arrangements." A good demonstration of this thesis is the government's—and the Alliance's—efforts in the touchy field of tax reform.

Chile has always lacked what the experts call a "tax climate," in which people pay their taxes either because they know they will be caught and punished if they don't, or because they know the taxes will be well used, once collected. The basic problem in Chile has been that the taxpayer has never felt that he got anything for his money. U.S. residents may gripe about paying taxes, but they know they will get something in return—schools, roads, public health services and a fair count. Until recently, Chileans have never had such assurances. When a people fails to pay its tax bill, it must pay a hidden tax. Parents must send their children to private schools because public schools are no good. They must pay higher prices for products because shipping over poor roads is costly. The Chileans—who have evaded a good 50 percent of their taxes over the years—respond that if they did pay up, the government would neither build schools nor improve roads, but hire another several thousands of its friends.

Government protestations that such practices will end have only limited effect. The certain remedy is a tax machinery so fair and effective that people will feel compelled to pay. It is this machinery that the Alliance (Chileans assisted by Americans) has sought to build.

Chile's income-tax law has been overhauled. Complex exemptions—shelters for the privileged—have been greatly reduced. Income from foreign sources has been made taxable, a measure designed to attack the erosion of Chilean capital into investments abroad. Tax rates have been altered; the effect has been to lower the bill for middle-income taxpayers, particularly professionals, and raise it considerably for those in the upper brackets. In some cases the taxes of the wealthy have doubled.

A major attempt has been made to assess the real value of properties in Chile. Old assessments were no more than 10 percent of market value, often much less. With the help of the OAS, a land cadaster was made; for the first time in history, Chile had an aerial map showing precise property lines. Data was also collected on soil capacity. Knowing who owned what and what the land could produce enabled authorities to triple the yield from agricultural properties. Similar reforms improved urban-area assessments by two and one-half times on the average. One Chilean who worked on the reforms was the nephew of a woman whose property was revalued at twenty times its old rate. He was afraid to show her the new rates.

A second major reform effort was the reorganization of collections. Before, many Chileans had never even bothered to hide their resources, because the administration of the tax system simply wasn't good enough to catch them. In 1962 Chile's tax collection agency had twenty-six individual departments reporting to its director. There was no delegation of authority. Work habits inhibited coordination. District offices lacked adequate leadership from the national offices. Each district, in effect, operated its own system. Many minor taxes cost more to administer than they yielded in revenue.

Under the direction of U.S. tax specialist Norman D. Nowak, the Tax Modernization Project set up a training department, reorganized the service itself, installed a buddy system (pairing newcomers with qualified tax agents), improved interior communications and organized an enforcement unit to investigate and help prosecute cases of fraud. Within a year Chile had its first tax fraud case in history in court; after a four-year struggle, a Chilean woman, the owner of a nightclub, was sentenced to jail for avoiding $3000 in taxes. She was probably the first person ever jailed in Latin America for income tax evasion. Other Chileans threatened with punishment resorted to the old tricks of delay and appeal, but a major scare had been thrown into Chile's elite society. Said Nowak: "If we can create a tax climate, the rest takes care of itself."

The figures would seem to bear him out. In 1963 tax collections rose 13.5 percent in real terms over 1962. Not only were Chileans beginning to pay their taxes, they were declaring more of their income. Chile stood to gain $150 million annually from the project.

The situation of the Alliance in Chile is, as one U.S. official put it, "light years better" than it was at the outset. And yet, the situation is not what it ought to be. Few Chileans identify with the Alliance. Aside from the professionals directly involved, *no* Latin American really feels that the Alliance is his program. Rather, it is a foreign aid program of the United States. Why is this? What went wrong?

There are several answers. Latin Americans, in general, suspect that the U.S. wants to tie Latin America to itself through the Alliance, as part of what they perceive as a continuing process of domination. They are understandably suspicious. It is little known in the U.S., but well known in Latin America, that a good portion of U.S. aid never really leaves the United States. The money "loaned" to a foreign government is used to pay American factories for American products, which are then shipped to the recipient. Other portions of assistance money are used to pay the salaries of U.S. technicians.

A second problem is that Latin American governments, by and large, have failed to produce dynamic programs of their own. They use the Alliance to fight crisis, not cause. Says Frei: "These countries and governments, completely taken up by their immediate problems, have eagerly taken money that permits them to save an emergency situation, rather than resources organized for development and transformation." Such bilateral accords between the U.S. and a troubled Latin American republic may be helpful, but unlike the Alliance they are not in the spirit of multilateral agreements to solve long-range problems.

The first two problems are historical and were inevitable; they can be solved in time. A third problem is one that should never have arisen. The diagnosis of the Latin American problem in the Punta del Este charter was excellent, but the timing it suggested could not have been less realistic. Centuries-old problems do not succumb at once. It was an American sense of urgency imposed upon a Latin American set of problems. When American journalists, promised immediate progress, did not see it, they pounced. Within months after the Alliance was launched, it was widely heralded as a failure.

I remember one particularly heartbreaking moment in

the process, a day in São Paulo, Brazil, where reporters had gathered to cover the second annual review meeting of the Alliance. I arrived just after noon of the first day, but others had arrived earlier, and the "line" was out: the Alliance for Progress was dead. It seemed all the more heartbreaking because many of the cynical reporters present had never visited an Alliance project. I asked one of them, a syndicated writer, if he too believed that the Alliance was dead. "Let's put it this way," he said. "The Alliance was stillborn." A while later a Brazilian journalist, a popular young fellow often consulted by other journalists for his views, approached. "You know the story of this conference?" he said. "The Alliance for Progress is dead, but everyone is afraid to write the obituary." Five minutes later a third journalist, who habitually depended upon the views of the second, whispered in my ear: "I am writing the obituary of the Alliance for Progress."

The predictions, of course, were self-fulfilling. The talk of failure permeated the system. By August 1965 the *Visión Letter*, easily the most sensitive weekly publication on Latin America available in the U.S., was compelled to make this mournful analysis:

> The fourth anniversary of the signing of the Alliance for Progress charter was met with a mood of defeatism in most hemisphere capitals. There was carping in former years, but there also was a buoyancy and some catch phrase for a new initiative—"multilateralization" or "integration" . . . Today, there seems to be no consensus on how to proceed, and a widespread frustration that the problems of semi-development are as burdensome as ever . . . Most inter-American thinkers agree that the Alliance has two problems: what is being done, and what people feel. The latter is important. The program has fallen on dog days because of a sinking morale. The loss of President Kennedy, with whose name the Alliance was emotionally linked, was a bad blow

and was confounded by the lack of communication between President Johnson and hemisphere leaders. It was further hurt by the feeling that the Vietnam war meant lessened interest in Latin America and again by disappointment over the intervention in the Dominican Republic. In brief, the program has lost its mystique with leaders, and with the Latin American peoples.

The article added this ironical summary:

No appraisal of the Alliance is ever completed without a list of solid accomplishments. During the first four years, according to Alliance figures, these include: 40 million people fed under the Food for Peace Program; close to 100,000 teachers trained; 26,000 classrooms constructed and 12 million textbooks distributed; 850 hospitals, clinics and mobile health centers put in service; more than 275,000 agricultural loans issued; more than 1000 water systems put in operation; almost 1900 credit unions and savings and loan associations created along with 27 development banks; 12,000 miles of roads paved, 8500 public administrators trained; and more than 300,000 private homes constructed. Impressive? Perhaps, but in Washington the above is called the annual laundry ticket. The requirements remain as staggering in 1965 as they were in 1961.

Obviously technological development alone is not enough. Something vital is missing. Reviewing the Alliance and its problems in 1965, Richard Eder of the *New York Times* offered a crucial clue. The development efforts will ultimately prove fruitless, he wrote,

. . . if the political relationships between Latin America and the United States degenerate. Any vigorous, politically secure government in Latin America must in the long run be able to tell its people what it thinks of the United States and why it collaborates with it. Right now there are some serious unanswered questions hindering such explanations. How much social change can occur before the United

States disapproves? How tidy do you have to be about your associates when you overthrow a military regime? How independent a foreign policy can you have before the United States stops aid? President Johnson's decision to take a more personal role toward Latin America is an important advance. But before real political progress can be made the President will have to convey the answers to some of these questions, and before he can do this, he will have to answer them for himself.

The heart of the relationship between states is no different that it is between individuals. We treat others in one of two ways—as objects, or as human beings. Either we use them, or we love them. Our approach determines their response. If we have a Latin American problem today, it is because we have not genuinely convinced the Latin Americans that we care about them as people. Rather, they believe—and with good reason—that our efforts in their behalf emanate from concern for ourselves.

Our response to the Dominican crisis, one Washington official observed at the time, represented "a feeling on the part of policy people that we've got to act like a big power." The feeling permeates our overall efforts. It originates in Washington, and there is almost nothing that U.S. officials on the spot can do to allay its effects.

It is a natural human reaction to expect those we help to support us when we need them. In the Dominican crisis we received criticism instead. Our highest officials were understandably angered. "What's the matter with that man down there?" one Washington policymaker was said to have demanded about Eduardo Frei. Laments one U.S. observer: "Washington is interested in short-run political interests: reward your friends, punish your enemies. It says, 'If these people don't co-operate, cut their water off. If Frei can't keep his mouth shut, let him go someplace else for his money.' It's an effort to apply to international politics what works in domestic politics."

Actually the remarks that aroused Washington most at the time were made not by Frei but by a subordinate. To condemn Frei for the statements of a critical Christian Democratic party official "who has spent thirty years thinking this way" would be like condemning President Johnson for "Wayne Morse's speeches in the Senate," this observer goes on. "The sign of maturity in leadership is that you can expect that sort of nonsense."

If the U.S. truly respected Latin Americans, it would realize that their "acting out" is a precise measure of our success. As one U.S. official put it: "If we create strong, viable societies, they will have the strength to be independent of the U.S."

Our goal should be unity, not unanimity. "A series of strong, healthy nations in the hemisphere doesn't harm us. Our adversaries can't take that," a U.S. aide declares. Admittedly that is risky business. But this is a time for taking risks in Latin America. Says another U.S. official: "If we don't, we're dead. We're only going to do well down here by doing the things that make it most uncomfortable for us. They may spit in our eye, but as long as they don't do anything seriously wrong, it won't be so bad. They're growing up, and we have to realize that they're going to act as people with new-found freedom and strength."

In Chile we are no longer guilty of overt power plays, if the words of Frei are to be believed. I once asked him whether the United States had ever used economic pressures to obtain political ends. His response was given so passionately that it could only be accepted as genuine:

I declare in the most categorical manner that I might, that neither in a direct nor an indirect manner, has the government of the United States insinuated any type of pressure. It has proceeded with the greatest discretion in making its arguments to us, and with the utmost respect for our feelings. In no moment have we had the remotest impression that this could possibly occur.

Yet much of our effort abroad seems to be characterized by a subtle psychological imperialism. We would like to have others do as we do, not so much because it has worked so well for us that we believe it will work elsewhere, but because unconsciously we seek the confirmation and gratification that accompany the validation of one's own ideas. We are allergic to independence where it does not vindicate our past.

And so we preach the doctrine of capitalism and free enterprise, little realizing that one major cause of contemporary Latin American dissatisfaction with the U.S. relates to a total misunderstanding of what capitalism is and does. The Latin American gets his ideas of capitalism from the manner in which it is practiced at home. As Fredrick Pike observes:

> So far as Chile's lower classes and reform leaders are concerned, capitalism has been synonymous with social injustice. When United States spokesmen continue to announce in Chile that all problems can be solved through free-enterprise capitalism, without making it clear that the form of capitalism in mind is not necessarily that practiced in Chile, they convince the reformers that the United States stands in opposition to basic social readjustments.

For capitalism to work, one needs first, a widely held democratic vision that is concretized by laws that are obeyed, and second, a habit of wide public ownership. Chile has had neither the habit nor the capacity. We must find the strength to help her develop both. We can caution,

when invited to, but we cannot let our prejudices dominate diplomacy. When we do, it is not only embarrassing
but destructive.

In 1965 the Special Operations Research Office, a U.S.
Army-financed institution affiliated with American University, launched an ill-conceived and ill-concealed project to
determine the capability for internal warfare of Chile's
leftist extremists. The Communist party newspaper, *El
Siglo*, unmasked the project after it had been alerted by
scholars contacted by a University of Pittsburgh professor.
The almost totally unfavorable reaction transcended party
lines. What provoked the Chileans was not only the semi-
clandestine nature of the inquiry, but the lack of confidence in Chile and the echoes of paternalism the inquiry
manifested. In the wake of the Dominican intrusion, the
more sensitive Chileans asked whether the U.S. was preparing for a landing of marines in Valparaíso in the event
Chilean affairs took a sharp turn to the left. U.S.-Chilean
relations had suffered one more unnecessary blow.

We must realize that Chile will in the next years seek
her own outlets, as will most other Latin American countries, and we must not try to stop them. We will only fail.
As *Latin American Trends* notes:

> Over the next decade Latin American countries are going
> to expand economic and political relations with the major
> Communist countries, and we have no choice but to let them
> gain their own experience in this field. If we try to block the
> development of their relations with the Soviet Union or Com-
> munist China, we will only add glamour to the Communist
> approaches and offers. There is nothing more educational
> for any ruling group than learning to deal with Communist
> governments. . . . We cannot object if the Soviet Union
> wants to become a major consumer of Latin American coffee.
> The change from tea to coffee might, indeed, add a very
> desirable stimulation to Soviet life. The more the Latin

American countries broaden their markets, the less they will be able to blame their economic difficulties on the U.S. alone. Soviet trade and aid by itself, without the presence of Soviet military power or a Castro-type seizure of power from within, has never added a single member to the Communist grouping, and Latin America, we must remember, is not exposed to direct strategic or political pressure by the Soviet Union or China.

Regardless of the stresses that a changing relationship creates, it is evident in a hundred different ways that the future of Chile is with the United States. "We need the U.S. financially and technically," explains Chile's ambassador to the OAS, Alejandro Magnet. "If we're against the U.S. we pass to the other side. We believe that an understanding with the U.S. is possible. Our objective is not to be coincident with the U.S., but complementary to it." The feeling is evident in the remark of Eduardo Frei as he returned to Chile from Europe: "Well, if we ever needed any demonstration that Chile's interest lies with the U.S., it was this trip." Comments one American: "The man who said this marched against the U.S. in 1954 over Guatemala (protesting U.S. interference there). The difference between him and others is that others are still marching."

Frei's feeling is overwhelmingly evident in his statements of record. In 1958 he wrote:

I think that no responsible person in Latin America can deny the fact that co-operation with the United States is of fundamental importance for this continent's economic development, its future prosperity, and the well-being of its peasant, industrial, and mining masses. If this co-operation does not exist, the masses of these countries are going to experience long years of bitter suffering and backwardness. Those who make use of hatred for strategic purposes are basically sacrificing their peoples. They are the counterpart of those who sell out (to the foreigner). . . . Those who really work for true friendship between Latin America and the United States are those who are proposing a policy of justice, frankness, and co-operation, on the basis not of weakness but of firmness in saying what is taking place. *It is necessary to convince the North American public that just as the workers of the United States have succeeded by a bitter struggle in arriving at a level of social justice without impeding progress, so also Latin America must by bitter struggle arrive at full international justice and real economic co-operation in defending its riches, in defending its workers, and in defending its life.* [my italics]

In the last sentence Frei reminds us of our common heritage and our common cause. The heritage is revolution, and the cause is the freedom in decency of man. George Lodge makes the point better than I:

> If the United States is to secure its vital interests in Latin America, it must better understand the nature of revolution there; it must determine more precisely its relationship and commitment to that revolution, and it must revise accordingly its Latin American policies and programs, both private and public.
>
> . . . By revolution we mean the deep and radical changes in the social, political and economic fabric of a nation or a people which proceed constantly underneath the chaos and the coups and reach into every phase of work and life. It is emotional and spiritual; it is concerned above all with dignity and justice; and in Latin America as well as elsewhere it appears to be inevitable, and in its high purposes eminently desirable. Latin America is in the process of choosing the direction in which the revolution proceeds, the particular ends it seeks, the priorities it gives to those ends and the degree to which it maintains its independence from outside powers. This revolution does not seem to require bloodshed or violence. It did in Mexico many years ago, but in Chile we appear to be watching it progress in peace and order.

What is missing from our attitude toward this revolution is a consistent and persistent sense of outrage at the conditions it attacks, offered with such passion that the Latin Americans will not doubt where we stand. We have forsaken, as Lodge points out, "the revolutionary nature of our own growth and development."

We cannot afford to be embarrassed by ideology. Rather, we must proclaim it. Says Lodge: "Let us not forget, in sum, that we are a revolutionary people; that in a real sense we made the word honorable; that we have more right to its noble use than do those who call themselves Communists."

The battle for Latin America turns on our ability to recapture that word from Castro. For that word, to the Latin American, is magic. To him it means change, and change is what he wants.

Castro's appeal to Latin Americans was never ideological; the overwhelming majority of Latin Americans have never found communism appealing. Yet for several years he remained a symbol, even as resentment of his dictatorship grew and admiration for him shriveled. The reason was simple: he changed something. He set out to do something and did it. To the young Latin American this is more than heart's blood. It is the heart itself. He is the child of failure in a world of achievement. Who can blame him? He wants to be a man. The world has now intruded upon the carefully styled structures of Latin America, advertising the means by which men these days are measured—by deeds, accomplishments, completed acts. To those who know what it is to be men, the fear of failure is like a threat to their lives. Latin Americans who decry the "capitalist imperialists" are not just complaining about profits that leave their country; every time they use a razor blade made by foreigners, it is a galling reminder that their own people are unable to do the job.

It has been said that Castro did us a favor. He awakened

us to the plight of Latin America. He did more. He revealed what it is that Latin America needs. It needs pride. It needs self-respect. It needs the confirming human experience of doing something for itself.

That, more than anything, is the importance of Chile in Latin America today. An indigenous victory, with an indigenous system, could charge the hemisphere. Eduardo Frei is a bridge between what is and what ought to be. As *Le Figaro*, the French newspaper wrote "The prestige now enjoyed by Mr. Frei in Latin America is the only effective rampart against the assault of Castroism. On the success or failure of Chile depends in great part the future orientation of the forces of progress in Latin America."

Freedom is not a gift. It is an achievement. Nowhere in the world, perhaps, is this better understood than in Chile.

Chile today is blessed with the best leaders it has ever had, plus a cadre of honest and passionate professionals. They are in a hurry for achievement; they are intolerant of restraints. Their efforts may produce a form of freedom somewhat different from our own, but if they succeed it will be freedom just the same.

In 1862, Lincoln called the American idea "the last, best hope of earth." In 1967 radical democracy would seem to be the last, best hope of Chile. That it is the single alternative to Marxism is the most significant lesson available in Latin America today.

One hundred and fifty years ago Símon Bolívar, momentarily beleaguered in his fight against Spanish tyranny, took asylum on the English island of Jamaica. There he wrote his *Letter from Jamaica*, analyzing his revolution. In it he offered this prophecy:

> If any American republic is to have a long life, I am in
> clined to believe it will be Chile. There, the spirit of liberty

has never been extinguished; the vices of Europe and Asia arrived too late, or not at all, to corrupt the customs of that distant corner of the world. . . . In a word, it is possible for Chile to be free.

Chile, with patience and dignity, has awaited her destiny. Perhaps, at last, it is here.

And Now ...

There has been no period in Chilean history comparable to the one through which the country passed in the months since this book was finished. A historic compact between government and private foreign enterprise was soldered; the economy roused itself; agricultural reform was passed into law; President Frei voluntarily refused stand-by budgetary assistance from the United States and other would-be benefactors—and he was imprisoned within his country's borders by a mindless act of pique, then disciplined by an election result that, among other things, revived the Marxists' hopes for the presidency in 1970.

In the last few weeks I have had the option of wedging these events into the body of the book or of including them in an afterword. I have chosen the latter course for two compelling reasons. The experience that makes a book should remain intact; the time in which it took place becomes one of its identifying factors. To chase events or modify positions because of these events serves neither the reader nor history. Secondly, I can think of no more illuminating way to measure the pace and scope of change than to cast the events of recent months against their historical source.

I am excited by these events—even those that on first consideration appear negative in character. Earlier, I had to straddle certain ground on the basis of information then available; I will not straddle that ground here. In September 1966, it seemed too early to say whether Frei would succeed. It is not too early now. One may argue with the form or content of change, but one cannot deny its existence. If Frei's one contribution to Chilean evolution is to cement the idea of change, then success can already be said to be his.

There are commentators now saying that Frei's unprecedented rebuff by the Chilean Senate, which refused to authorize his February 1967 trip to the United States, invalidated his credentials as a model Latin American reformer. I could not disagree more. I cannot imagine a more revealing expression of frustration than the one concocted by Frei's opponents last January. Defeated at almost every turn by Frei, unable to break his rigid adherence to principle through legislative barter, they unearthed an obscure constitutional provision requiring that both houses of Congress approve a presidential trip from the country: the Senate, by a vote of 23 to 15, kept Frei from making an eight-day official visit to the United States, scheduled for early February. Conservative and rightist-nationalist senators said they voted against the trip because President Johnson, in referring to the Christian Democratic campaign slogan "revolution with liberty" in his pre-visit statement, had "intervened" in Chilean affairs. The Marxists said that in keeping Frei from the United States, they were protesting against the war in Vietnam. But there was no doubt in anyone's mind that these were stories for public consumption.

I view the rebuff as an act of embittered men—property owners whose unproductive yet speculatively profitable lands would be taken by reform; Marxist reformers whose thunder Frei has stolen. Their curious compact hurt Frei, but it hurt Chile more. The *New York Times* noted editorially:

> Eduardo Frei, Chile's and Latin America's first Christian Democratic president, had become too important. This, plus the old Latin tradition of suspecting statesmen who are on especially friendly terms with Washington, seems to be the main reason for the Chilean Senate's refusal to allow the President to visit the United States.
>
> It was a shocking exhibition of raw politics on the part of the Senate majority in Chile. President Frei's proposed trip to the United States would have added to Chile's prestige— but also to President Frei's. This was just what the politicians did not want to see. The chief culprits are the once-dominant Radicals, a center party now split into left and right wings.
>
> The traditional left, Socialist and Communists, could have been expected to vote against the President. Because of Mr. Frei's "revolution with liberty" which includes a modest agrarian reform, the right-wing liberal and conservative parties were also glad to strike a blow. It was the old business of politics making strange bedfellows.
>
> But the real reason of the Senate vote was to humiliate the Chilean president. In the process, the opposing Senators have humiliated their own country.

The incident dramatized Frei's problems. But the point that must not be lost is that it also dramatized his progress.

The frustration of his opponents powerfully suggests that Frei could be on the verge of something more than comprehensive reform in Chile; he could be about to demonstrate that democratic institutions can serve revolutionary needs.

The more I have thought about it the more I have come to view the night Frei stood down the four senators who came to bargain with him—their support for his copper bill in exchange for his consent to a more generous remuneration for expropriated lands—as a transcendent moment in Chilean affairs. More than a copper bill was at stake here; it was a confrontation between the future and the past. At some point, this confrontation had to be made. No Chilean president had ever faced down the Establishment before in such fashion or on such an issue. None had really cared to; most were either of the Establishment to begin with, or embraced by them before they had finished. Frei broke the Establishment's clasp.

The copper bill became law. Now Frei can create the revenues he needs to finance his programs. Now he can solve his chronic dollar problems. Now he can eliminate the worst cause of friction between the United States and Chile—foreign exploitation of Chilean natural resources. Said the *New York Times*: "Chileanization of the industry is a victory for common sense, good neighborliness and sound economics." From the outset Frei's strategy had been to make copper—his country's chief resource, and one from which she had previously received a poor share—the springboard for her economic and social take-off. Here are just a few of the effects:

• The country's annual balance of payments deficit, which averaged $200 million a year between 1959 and 1964, and $45 million in 1965 and 1966, has now been eliminated, and will remain so as long as the demand and price for copper remain high. This year Chile will actually earn a surplus, perhaps $100 million. This was the situation that prompted Frei

223

to issue his fiscal declaration of independence prior to his anticipated trip to Washington. Under its terms Chile will neither seek nor accept international credits or loans to help balance its budget in 1967; nor will the country require the usual annual "stand-by" fund to support the value of the Chilean escudo during this year. Chile *will* continue to receive loans to finance its overall development program, but these loans presumably would be repaid on schedule without disturbing the country's hard-currency position. Chile's progress, Frei was saying, would be bought by Chile. The psychological component of this fiscal success is incalculable but profound.

Without question, the improvement in the balance of payments picture was occasioned by the dramatic upturn in the price of copper. But those who dismiss this as a fluke should reflect again. There have been such times in the past, but the foreign exchange always went into the purchase of expensive luxury items for the few. Now it was being used to retire debts and to finance future industrial expansion.

• New investments of $530 million are beginning to flow into Chile. They will double copper output by 1970 to more than one million tons a year. While the present exceedingly high price of copper may drop, total revenues would still increase due to larger imports.

• Profits from the expansion will soon be felt in increased demand throughout the economy. Economists are forecasting a real Gross National Product growth of 5 percent a year through 1970; industrial expansion, they say, will increase at a rate of 7 percent.

• Private industry, calculating the impact, appears ready to commit itself at last. Many entrepreneurs, fearing socialism, had remained all but dormant; now, foreseeing profits,

224

they planned to expand. Of 174 firms responding to a government query last summer, 130—75 percent—said they anticipated important increases in production later that year or in 1967; of the 92 firms that volunteered specifics, the average increase was 42 percent. New industries or significant additions to existing industries were in cellulose, petrochemicals, automobiles, iron and steel, fishing, sugar-beet refining, phosphates, fertilizer, tires, sewing machines, copper-wire drawing and electronics.

Even before the copper agreement was a certainty the economic indicators had begun to improve. Cast against their position in previous years they all looked marvelous. Total production increased an average of 3.7 percent annually between 1955 and 1964; in 1963 and 1964 it dipped to 2.6 percent which, after accounting for population increase, is nil. But for 1965 and 1966, the first two years of Frei's administration, total production increased by 7.4 percent yearly—more than triple the preceding two-year period. Inflation, which depreciated currency values by an average of 48 percent in each of the two years preceding the Frei administration, was held to 25.9 percent in 1965 and something under 20 percent in 1966. (The official figure is 18 percent.) The 1966 figure was a disappointment—the Frei people had hoped to get it down to 15 percent. But economists are predicting that this target could be achieved in 1967, and that it would be reasonable to aim for a 10 percent annual increase thereafter. In a hot economy, that is considered a normal and tolerable rate.

There has been a general rise in well-being for the majority of Chileans, due somewhat to the curb on inflation, but also to wage increases provoked by the government; workers, particularly farm workers, are 25 percent better off today than they were before Frei took office. There has been a redistribution in income; people who had little or no money before now have money—and the things that it buys.

In education the Frei administration was able to augment enrollment in its first year in office by appropriating for schools a sum equal to the average of the amount allowed for the previous five years. "We are more than meeting our objectives," Frei wrote me in November 1966. Statistics tell the happy story: 11,000 new classrooms; 230,000 new students; 6000 new teachers. Children who once had to drop out of school after the sixth grade because places in the higher grades were reserved for the brighter students now can stay on through the eighth or ninth grades. Children who never had schools have them now.

In housing the government almost doubled the previous government's pace for a while, even though housing had been that administration's major program. Housing starts continue at a diminished but substantial rate.

Such progress moved Lewis H. Diuguid, a 1965 Alicia Patterson Fund fellow on leave from the Washington *Post*, to observe just prior to the Senate's veto of Frei's proposed visit: "President Eduardo Frei of Chile will arrive in Washington February 1, as welcome as any guest that the U.S. government is ever likely to receive from Latin America. He is a personification of the Alliance for Progress, a tax-collecting idealist who already has shattered the tradition of official visits by declaring beforehand that he would no longer need the hosts' massive budget aid."

Problems, mistakes, anguish, criticism, even disillusion have been companions of progress. Some of the situations have been ironically comic. One recalls Juan de Onis' account in the *New York Times* of a dinner party at which a conservative businessman pointed an accusing finger at

U.S. ambassador Ralph Dungan and said, "This country is being led to social chaos and you are to blame." But most of the problems are substantial. Lack of administrative experience, the incapacity of some government officials, planning shortcomings, and poor legislative strategy have all been evident in some degree.

Deflationary pressures create an uncertain new world for businessmen used to borrowing for their needs, then paying their debts with depreciated money. Chilean consumers are annoyed because they are used to buying on credit and seeing inflation reduce their debts. Tight credit makes expansion difficult; that is annoying. The middle-class white-collar worker, particularly the civil servant, sees prices continue to rise, (if more slowly now) but his own wage is carefully controlled to allow a barely offsetting increase, and he gets annoyed. These are the normal symptoms that attend any cure following an inflationary binge. Inevitably, the average man, lost in economic theory, knows only what is happening now and heavily discounts the value to him of more stable money a year or two from now.

Politically the Christian Democrats have not solidified their own party, principally because they have failed to deal with an inherent contradiction. The party's centrists, among whom the president is numbered, believe that private enterprise, carefully controlled, must play a vital role in Chile's future; the party's leftists reject capitalism altogether, and their attacks upon it serve to chill the very industrialists upon whom the leadership counts. Another major disappointment has been the party's ineptness in organizing urban workers or wresting control of major unions from the Marxist FRAP.

In the fall of 1966 Chile distressed her liberal friends by ordering twenty-one British Hawker Hunters at a cost of $15 million. What provoked the order was the delivery earlier to Argentina of twenty-five A-4B Skyhawks, bought from the United States for $250,000 each. Newspapers—even those that deplored the purchase—correctly identified Chile's historic problems with Bolivia and Argentina. They also noted Chile's understandable concern over recent political events in Argentina, where the constitutional regime of Arturo Illia was overthrown by General Onganía. What the accounts inexplicably failed to recall was a serious border incident in 1965 that provoked the Argentines to threats of war. Given that country's mood of frustration, there was no telling what would happen. Nonetheless, the incident left a sour taste that even these reasons could not remove.

The principal criticism of Frei, as Diuguid—whose recent reports from Chile have been as comprehensive and objective as any coming from the country—points out, is from the more fundamentalist reformers, whose ranks include young university professors and foundation specialists, as well as Christian Democratic militants. The burden of their charge is that while Frei has proved himself an excellent economic technician he has shown little taste for meaningful social change. They believe that his failure to utilize his political weapons was the cause of the failure of a bill to give legal status to the base organizations of *Promoción Popular*, and they feel that this aspect of Frei's program has been the least successful of all.

Because it represents the most serious and most surprising challenge to Frei, the criticism of the non-Marxist Left deserves careful consideration. Herewith, Diuguid's digest of this view:

> President Frei has proved to be a competent economic reformer, using wisely the country's windfall profits from the high price of copper. But Frei and his party came to power

in 1964 under a pledge for fundamental change in a nation of 9 million people that had ossified economically because it was hopelessly stratified socially. While the Revolution was to consist of many specifics—agrarian reform, a government share in the copper exploitation previously dominated by U.S. capital, defeat of disruptive inflation—a key general objective was to organize the voiceless lower half of the population for active participation in government and society.

But, the critics say, the President has given up revolution in favor of control—wage settlements without strikes, salary readjustments without inflation, legislation with the approval but not the unsettling participation of Congress. His desire for order has precluded effective attempts to organize the bypassed masses, a process that is of course disorderly. To these critics the President is, in short, an ideal reformist leader for a calm developed state. Frei would make a fine gringo statesman, was the way one economist put it. But they are not convinced that this qualifies him for the quite different problems of a developing nation, and by extension they are doubtful that the Frei way is meaningful to other Latin American countries.

For these critics, the Revolution was to have been a quick, thorough reordering of the social structure. And while it was to have been in relative liberty, it was bound to be disruptive if not violent to the upper classes from which had to come the means for bettering the lot of the lower ones. The critics now look about them and say that the old order has not changed. Peasant wages have doubled from nearly nothing, and the upper classes are paying significant amounts of taxes for the first time, yet the old patterns of economic and social, and to a lesser extent political, power remain the same. The voice of the technocrat is heard in the land, and the social revolutionaries have lost the President's attention.

As Diuguid states, these arguments are subject to endless qualification. His own are included in his final report for the Alicia Patterson Fund* and will, I hope, later be

* Reform, Revolution and Frei, by Lewis H. Diuguid, The Alicia Patterson Fund, January 7, 1967.

part of a book on his year in Chile. He praises Frei for the president's statesman-like refusal to succumb to political pressures and ease up on anti-inflationary restrictions, an act that would win him back much wavering middle-class support; and for his belief that "in social development, the piper must be paid before he plays, in hard currency . . . with all its foreign aid, the job is Chile's." But Diuguid concludes with a nod to the new intellectual and professional critics. "So far the Frei policies do not make a revolution—unless it be argued that the true reform policy is so rarely applied in Latin America as to be revolutionary by its very existence."

I would so argue, and I believe it is important to do so here, inasmuch as it is generally agreed that the issues being decided in Chile are hemispheric—and perhaps even global—in significance.

The dispute centers on the style or content of change, but not on the fact of change itself. The critics must concede that while change may not be fast enough or thorough enough for them, change is underway. The three elements of the government's program cited above—"agrarian reform, a government share in the copper exploitation previously dominated by U.S. capital, defeat of disruptive inflation"—have all been achieved in part or in full. It is my view that the cities do not sufficiently appreciate the social impact of economic change. Social and economic reforms reinforce one another. If one attacks an outmoded land structure, he does so to improve production—an economic end. But he also does so in order to deliver justice to 250,000 peasant families whose existence in previous times was all but unrecognized. This is a social end. To what extent is a man's belief in himself for the first time in his life—a social goal—caused by his recognition as a paying member of a money economy? The phenomena are different, but inseparable.

I have never met a politician more intent on social change than Frei. But the president, with a keen sense of timing, is using economic change as one means of initiating it. He might very well succumb to pressures and concentrate on populist measures. But certain aspects of social change are economically counterproductive in the short run. Hospitals and schools are humane and necessary, but money to pay for them must be diverted from projects that provide earnings and taxes. Frei's housing program had to be curtailed recently when it was found to be adding too much heat to the economy.

Frei's critics contend that while he has brought reform aplenty to Chile, he is no revolutionary. They argue with his choice of the word. Frei's "revolution in liberty" means precisely what it says: change in a democratic setting. The critics suggest that Frei reveals the moderate's mentality when he fails to call the peasants to action, and urge them to seize the land. He never said he would. His argument— his life—rests on the conviction that democratic institutions are perfectly sufficient to reorder an unjust society. All they lacked in the past was use. Frei once quoted Jacques Maritain, in whom he has found much of his own strength: "Democracy may be uncouth, slow and defective, but democracy is the only road over which must pass the progressive energies of human history." His critics should realize by now that Frei means what he says.

In November 1966, Frei wrote me: "The government has estimated that some obstacles and reverses constituted a price that was necessary to pay, since it considers that it is very important not to break the democratic continuity of the nation and not to fall into any type of totalitarian adventure." His sense of pace and priority does not in any way appease his taste for change.

The critics speak of order as an evil and insist that change requires a disruptive process. That is Latin and romantic, but being both does not make it inevitable. The broad strokes and swift slashes of the hot-blooded social reorganizers invariably produce a violent reaction. I am not at all certain that the Latin American setting can stand such a pace. A "revolution in liberty" presumably means liberty for everyone. But given the Latin temperament, disorderly change can ultimately run wild. Cuba is an example now tattered from overuse. I offer Brazil in 1963 and 1964, where I watched a just, necessary and orderly process of social change captured and ruined by demagogues. Those democrats who know and love Brazil wince at the price now being paid.

The critics of Frei do not appreciate what a great conceptual change—or what a striking blow for change, per se— the economic reform of Chile's basic industry represented. Agrarian reform will follow, and eventually bank reform. So, too, will the lower class be organized and mobilized. It is not a question of disposition. It is simply a question of time.

That question, thanks to the municipal elections of 1967, has become the most delicate one confronting Eduardo Frei today.

Under normal circumstances, a municipal campaign is a poor field to test the growth of national political trends. Local elections are almost always determined by local problems and relationships. But the circumstances of this election were anything but normal. Stung by the Senate's rebuff in January 1967, Frei retaliated with a demand for a constitutional amendment that would permit dissolution of Congress and allow new elections at once. Chile's staggered system of alternately electing twenty and twenty-five senators every four years had left the country with a Senate that did not express the national will; in the 1965 elections the Christian Democrats had captured twelve Senate seats, making their total thirteen in all, but they remained badly outnumbered. Extremists at Right and Left could—and did—frustrate the president.

Many senators approved Frei's constitutional amendment. But the vote lacked a quorum. Sponsors of the bill planned to resubmit it to the Senate from the Chamber of Deputies; opponents of the bill would then have to muster a two-thirds vote to reject it. The thirteen Christian Democrats needed only three allies to see the amendment through—votes they could easily obtain if the party could prove it continued to possess a strong national mandate.

There are people close to Frei who insist that the election was enlarged at the insistence of party professionals, and that Frei himself had been reluctant to participate, knowing perhaps, as the *Visión Letter* pointed out in a postmortem, that no national leader can transfer his political appeal to local candidates—particularly if he is not on the ticket himself. Nonetheless, Frei committed the prestige of the presidency to the campaign. He traveled through the country, reciting the accomplishments of his administration. Such were the political conditions in the spring of 1967 that impartial observers believed the Christian Democrats must pull 42.3 percent of the total vote—equal to their proportion of the 1965 legislative vote—simply to hold their own.

The loss was greater than anyone had foreseen—even discounting the normal attrition in popularity of the party in power. The Christian Democrats polled 830,000 votes (36.5 percent of the total vote) against 995,000 in 1965.

All other parties gained. The Radicals moved from 312,000 (13.3 percent) in 1965 to 377,000 (16.4 percent) in 1967; the Nationalist Party (Conservatives and Liberals combined) from 309,000 (14.4 percent) to 330,000 (14.6 percent); the Socialists from 241,000 (10.2 percent) to 322,000 (14.3 percent) and the Communists from 290,000 (12.4 percent) to 354,000 (15.1 percent).

Local issues aside, the election underscored two present trends in Chilean political thought—each pivotal to the 1970 election, each moving in an opposite direction, but in both cases, away from Frei.

There is a sizable group in Chile for whom the municipal elections were an opportunity to express their resentment at what they perceived as a too rapid pace of change. This was the interpretation put upon the election result by the editorialists of the *New York Times*:

> There was resentment—among workers over wage controls and higher prices, among the middle class over higher taxes, among the landowners over the proposed agrarian reform, among the upper classes because of a certain inflexibility and refusal to make compromises on President Frei's part. Chileans, whom many consider the most democratic of all Latin Americans, are accustomed to the adjustments and the give-and-take of party politics. In the Frei regime they faced a stiffness that many considered to be arrogance.
>
> Eduardo Frei may have made his mistakes, but he is as intelligent, courageous and high-minded as any statesman in Latin America. He is suffering politically because he has been trying to make much-needed reforms too quickly . . .

Austerity is no picnic, and it is not very comprehensible. Without question, one of Frei's major problems is the middle-class office worker, civil servant and shopkeeper whose instincts are good but whose references are changing and whose budget is tight. In one of the more unfortunate

234

political coincidences of recent years, the week preceding the election was the deadline for paying stiff new personal and property taxes.

It is perfectly conceivable that some of the surge in support for the Marxists also represented a protest against the discomfort of austerity measures and fiscal controls. But it is more than likely that the vote for the Marxists was an indication of a second strong political trend in Chilean thought today—a feeling articulated by militant, but non-Marxist, leftist intellectuals that Frei is not acting swiftly enough.

The Radical and Nationalist vote together, which can be taken as a protest against too rapid change, increased 86,000, or 3.6 percent. The Socialist and Communist vote, which is more than likely a protest against too little change, increased 145,000, or 6.6 percent. While the vote for the Marxists is subject to much more subtle analysis, any subsequent study should not exclude the crude indication that there is political power behind the thirst for change, and that this power will continue to increase as suffrage spreads.

How Frei responds to these tugs upon his arms could affect the outcome of the presidential election in 1970. But it would be a mistake to suggest on the basis of one election —and a municipal election at that—that political thought in Chile is now polarizing. The breakaway vote is significant, but the consensus rests with Frei. His party is still more than twice as large as any other; it can count on 830,000 "chemically pure" adherents; this total is better than 100,000 votes more than that of the Communists and Socialists combined, and it still enjoys greater support by itself than any possible political combination. Even though the Christian Democrats lost numerical support, they nonetheless elected 649 local officials, against 327 for the Radicals, 260 for the Nationalists, 197 for the Socialists and 149 for the Communists.

Dissatisfaction is the shadow of change. It will lengthen as change enlarges. But change, not its shadow, is reality.

"The Frei administration has sparked a process of fundamental change which will be difficult to control and more difficult still to reverse," an able reviewer of the Chilean scene summarized recently. "If this process successfully runs its course, it will enhance Chile's modernization, create institutions for a more just and stable society and strengthen its constitutional order . . . Considering that the past two years represented a period of transition and adjustment, the Frei administration has made convincing progress (some of it very impressive) toward . . . a mutually reinforcing relationship between reforms, stabilization and development in order to attain a high and sustained rate of economic growth and social progress with a strengthened democratic order." A "revolution in liberty" could hardly ask for more.

Paris, May 1, 1967

INDEX

ABOUT THE AUTHOR

Leonard Gross joined the staff of *Look* magazine as a
senior editor in 1959. Two years later he went to
South America for an assignment that lasted over two
years and involved more than 100,000 miles of travel.
While there, he studied and wrote extensively on the
effects of Communism, Catholicism, and nationalism
on South America, as well as on the political impact
of the American business presence there. It was during
these two years that he first met and interviewed
Eduardo Frei, then a Chilean senator.

Mr. Gross received his B.A. from U.C.L.A. in 1949, and
a M.S. in journalism from Columbia University.
Before joining the staff of *Look*, he had had ten
years of journalistic experience working for such
publications as the *San Francisco Chronicle*, the *Wall
Street Journal*, *Collier's*, and in doing free-lance
writing. Altogether Mr. Gross has written more than
two hundred articles and stories for many well-known
commercial magazines. In addition to his book
God and Freud, he has collaborated on another
entitled *The Self in Pilgrimage*.